crochet FOR BEARS TO wear

more than 20 perfect projects for your favorite teddies and friends

amy o'neill houck

POTTER
CRAFT

New York

CONTENTS

Introduction 4

Meet the Bears 5

chapter 1
getting started

Taking Measurements **7**

How to Use the Patterns **8**

Special Techniques **11**

Tools **14**

chapter 2
out of hibernation

Spring Cleaning T-Shirt and Jeans **18**

7th Inning Stretch Baseball Jersey, Cap, Bat, and Ball **24**

Bear-y Pickin' Dress and Bonnet **32**

chapter 3
heat wave

Endless Summer Board Shorts **38**

California Dreamin' Bikini **42**

Gone Fishing Vest **46**

chapter 4
back to school

Show Your Colors Varsity Jacket and Book Bag **52**

Schoolgirl Pleated Skirt and Beret **60**

Let's Dance Ensemble **64**

chapter 5
staying warm in winter

Cozy Turtleneck **74**

Fair Isle Sweater **78**

Long Winter's Nap Nightgown and Cap **82**

Fisherman's Sweater **88**

Abbreviations 92

Resources 93

Acknowledgments 94

Index 95

INTRODUCTION

As I write another book about dressing your favorite teddy bears, dolls, and other fuzzy friends, I'm sitting in Alaska where real bears are a part of everyday life. So it is with a new understanding of bears and their surroundings that I bring you *Crochet for Bears to Wear*. In these pages we follow three special teddies through the seasons with projects for every kind of weather and activity—from cleaning out the den in spring to salmon fishing in summer, hitting the books in fall, and getting ready for hibernation in winter. In all, you'll find more than twenty quick-to-crochet garments and accessories to keep any stylish bear in vogue.

Of course, this book isn't just a book of clothing for toys. It's also a primer on crochet techniques and design—without a human-sized commitment. Clothes for bears and toys are small and portable, and many work up in just an evening or two. As such, these projects provide a fun introduction to a wide range of techniques and garment constructions. You'll learn seamless top-down crochet, crocheted ribbing, unusual starts and finishes to garments, lace, colorwork,

Aran crochet, and so much more. It just may happen that after you've worked a teddy bear–sized technique, you'll be inspired to incorporate your newly-learned skill into crochet projects of all shapes and sizes. All of the patterns in *Crochet for Bears to Wear* are easily custom-fit. Like people, no two teddies or toys are the same size, and you'll be able to adapt each pattern in this book to suit the measurements of your bear, doll, or other soft critter. Conceivably, you could even use the patterns to make clothes for a small child. You'll begin by learning how to measure your toy and how to use the customizing sidebars to make each pattern fit perfectly. You can also substitute

yarns as you wish. Many projects use just one or two skeins, making this book great for stash-busting.

As you become familiar with the customizing sidebars, you'll feel more comfortable making creative choices and changes, not just to the patterns on these pages, but also to your crocheting in general. What you hold in your hands is more than a book on crocheting teddy bear or doll clothes. It's a guide to an innovative style of garment design. My hope is that as you work each pattern, you'll gain the confidence and inspiration to develop your own creations.

Joey

Pearl

Eddie

MEET THE BEARS

If you're a knitter as well as a crocheter, you may have met Joey, Pearl, and Eddie in their debut book, *Knits for Bears to Wear*. Then, as now, these three teddies were the muses and models for the projects. Joey, an old family friend, was kind enough to introduce me to his buddies Eddie and Pearl. This brother-sister duo began life as Tofu Bears at Southwest Trading Company, which, in addition to raising young bears, makes yarn from many unusual plant fibers. It seemed fitting to use bears born at a yarn company; after all, they're no strangers to lovely handmade clothes. All three bears fit into the standard teddy size range (16–18" [40.5–45.5cm] tall), and, thankfully, they love to dress up.

Pearl has a penchant for pink and loves dresses and skirts. She also loves to accessorize. Naturally, she's excited that crochet lends itself well to hats and bags.

Pearl's brother, Eddie, will take any opportunity to dress down. As clothing is optional for bears, he'll just throw on what's most comfortable at the time—swim trunks for a day at the beach or a sweater to head out in the snow.

Joey is Eddie's best friend, but unlike his buddy he looks forward to dressing for every occasion—he has the right vest for fishing and favorite T-shirt and jeans for everyday wear.

What Joey, Eddie, and Pearl love best is playing dress-up in every season of the year. I hope they'll inspire you to create projects for the fuzzy friends you know.

chapter 1

GETTING *started*

MEASUREMENT CHART

Head Circumference:

_____

Neck Circumference:

_____

Neck Width (back of toy):

_____

Shoulder Width (edge to edge):

_____

Chest Circumference:

_____

Chest Width (between the arms):

_____

Belly Circumference (at the widest point):

_____

Arm Length (from shoulder to paw):

_____

Leg Length (from leg join to bottom of foot):

_____

Inside Leg Measurement (from top inseam to foot):

_____

Body Length (from base of the neck to the foot):

_____

If you're like me, you probably want to dive right in to the projects and start crocheting. But before you do, take a moment to learn how the unique pattern style in *Crochet for Bears to Wear* works. You'll get some practice measuring your bear to make sure your garment fits just right, and you'll learn how to read the patterns and use the customizing sidebars. I'll also explain any special techniques you might need for the projects in the book and discuss the tools you'll want to have handy.

TAKING MEASUREMENTS

If you stand Eddie and Joey side by side, you'll notice that although they're practically the same height, they have different proportions. Joey is more slender overall than Eddie, whose ears stick out farther, and who has a longer, wider snout. Much to Pearl's chagrin, all the bears in her family are a bit wide through the hips. The proportions are all elements to consider when crocheting a garment, so even if your doll or toy is 16–18" (40.5–45.5cm) tall, you'll want a few other measurements and you may need to make adjustments while you work.

NOT JUST FOR BEARS

Even though Pearl, Eddie, and Joey are my featured creatures, you can use this book as a guide to making clothes for almost any toy. Popular 18" (45.5cm) dolls are different in proportion to teddy bears, but close enough in size that many of the bears' patterns can be made for them without much modification. Does your child have a favorite doll? Use the customizing sidebars to make her a nightgown or sweater. Accessories like the bags and hats are some of the easiest patterns to resize. Maybe you'd like to make matching backpacks (page 57) for your son and his dinosaur, or a beret (page 60) for your daughter and one for her bunny rabbit. My daughter is begging me to make her a Fair Isle sweater—just like the one Eddie's wearing on page 78.

First, gather your materials and find a clean, flat surface on which to measure. You'll need a flexible measuring tape, a pencil, and a notebook or a measurement chart like the one on page 7. You can photocopy this chart to keep track of measurements for all your toys. As you fill in the chart, be sure that you are measuring from "point to point." For example, to measure arm length, place one end of the measuring tape at the shoulder or arm join and measure to the bottom of the paw. To properly measure circumference, make sure you take that measurement at the widest part on your bear or toy. The chart on page 7 comprises the basic measurements you'll need to customize the patterns in this book.

HOW TO USE THE PATTERNS

You'll notice that each set of instructions begins with a skill designation. These indicate the amount of concentration needed to work on a specific pattern. Patterns marked *Easy* are good for beginners; more advanced crocheters will find that the *Easy* patterns can be worked without too much concentration, making them perfect for stitching in a social setting or while watching television. *Intermediate* patterns require more focus and a few more skills than the *Easy* patterns, but beginners will be able to manage them with the help of the Special Techniques section on page 11. *Advanced* patterns are those best worked on in a quiet room. They require careful attention, and, if you're a beginner, perhaps the help of a more experienced crocheter.

The patterns are made up of two parts: a traditional crochet pattern for a 16–18" (40.5–45.5cm) bear, and a customizing sidebar. If your toy is close in size to our models, Joey, Eddie, and Pearl, you may find that just a few easy adjustments make for a perfect fit. Most adjustments won't involve multiple calculations, but they will require that you know your toy's proportions. Here's how to get started:

• **Compare the Finished Measurements of the garment you've chosen with your toy's measurements.** Make a note of any differences.

• **Read through the entire pattern to get an idea of what is required.** If you come across any techniques with which you're unfamiliar, check the front of the pattern and the Special Techniques section (page 11) for more information, or refer to a basic how-to-crochet book if necessary.

• **Choose your yarn and hook.** Each pattern suggests a yarn and a corresponding hook size for best results. You can easily make yarn substitutions as desired—just be sure to match your yarn to a hook size that will achieve the gauge given in the pattern. For help with yarn substitutions and hook sizes, turn to Resources on page 93. Further information on the yarns used in the patterns also can be found there.

• **Make a generous, six-inch (15 cm) swatch.** Crocheting a big swatch has a couple of purposes. First, it gives you time to test out the stitch pattern and your choice of hook. If you don't like the resulting fabric, change hooks until you do. Second, it gives you an adequate amount of fabric to take a good measurement of your chosen gauge.

• **Block your swatch.** Put your swatch through whatever rigors you imagine will befall the final garment. If the swatch is lace, wet block it by soaking the piece in tepid water and then gently squeezing out excess water. Stretch and pin the piece to a solid surface (a mattress covered by a towel works well), and allow it to dry. If you don't think the garment will need much blocking, you should at least stretch and manipulate your swatch to even the stitches.

This will allow you to figure the most accurate gauge possible.

• **Take careful measurements of your stitch gauge.** After blocking your swatch and laying it flat, place a ruler across the center of your swatch. Align the beginning of the ruler with the edge of one stitch and, without stretching the work, count the number of stitches within four inches (10 cm). Include half stitches if necessary; you can round up or down later as directed. Remember: if you plan to crochet the sample pattern without modification you'll need to match the gauge listed to achieve the correct size of the final project. Some customizing sidebars may ask you to record your row gauge. To do so, simply count the numbers of rows in a four-inch (10 cm) section of your swatch.

• **Refer back to your notes about sizing differences.** Each pattern has one measurement that determines the size of the foundation chain in the pattern. This is noted as the Key Measurement. If your toy's key measurement is different from what's listed, you'll want to use the customizing sidebars to create your garment. If your toy is about the same size as the model and the key measurement is the same, then you may just want to make a few small adjustments, like to the arm length or torso length. With a few noted exceptions, the sleeves and legs are crocheted from the top down, so you can easily adjust length.

Using the Customizing Sidebars

If you've decided to use the customizing sidebars, grab your calculator, measuring tape, notepad, and pencil, and find a quiet spot to make your pattern adjustments. Before making any changes, it's essential to have read and understood the pattern, so your calculations and changes make sense. The calculations will determine the size of your foundation chain, adjustments to length, and other proportions.

Often, a sidebar will refer back to the main pattern for a while, then ask you to do another calculation or make an adjustment. Use a sticky note to keep track of where you are in the pattern so you don't lose your place while moving back and forth. If the pattern requires a chain that's a multiple of a given number, the sidebar will tell you how to adjust the results of your calculations. For most patterns it will not matter whether you round up or down in your calculations. If rounding will affect a pattern, the instructions will specify whether to round up or down.

As you learn to customize a pattern, you'll become proficient in thinking about the relationships between gauge and measurement, and you'll see that within the confines of a pattern, there's lots of room for creativity. Essentially, each part of a garment, be it the back or a sleeve, is a geometric shape that gets filled in with a stitch pattern. Therefore, you need a certain number of stitches to make the pattern fit correctly within the confines of that shape. So if your gauge is different from the given pattern gauge, you'll need to make adjustments to make the stitch pattern fit into the shape. Usually this can be done by going up or down a hook size until the swatch meets the given pattern gauge. However, as you change the size of that geometric shape to fit your toy, you may need to adjust your stitch count. With a little math (provided for you in the customizing sidebars), your new design will fit the original geometry of the project.

Using Schematics and Charts

As you work the patterns, you'll notice that most include detailed schematics representing the size and shape of the project. Schematics allow you quickly to take in all the parts of a project—from the length of a sleeve to the garment's assembly to the direction of the stitches.

Schematics can also be helpful when you're customizing a project. The visual guide will allow you to imagine and make note of what you want to do differently. If you're changing stitch patterns, you might find it useful to crochet to the measurements listed on the schematic instead of a row count or stitch count given in the pattern. Schematics can be a great help for blocking— just use the given measurements as a guide.

A few patterns in the book include stitch or color charts. Charts use symbols as visual representations of stitches. They can be used in place of written row-by-row instructions or in conjunction with them. Many people find charts helpful when visualizing how a crochet stitch pattern or motif is made. Each chart includes a key to its stitch symbols, but if you've never read a chart before, you may need to consult a beginning crochet book for additional guidance.

Charts for work that is crocheted flat (back and forth) begin on a right-side row and are read from right to left, like your crochet, on the right-side rows. (The right side is the "public" side of the fabric.) When you turn the work, you begin to work a wrong-side row, so the chart row is read from left to right, as if the right side were always facing you.

Crochet motifs that are worked in the round, such as those in Pearl's Let's Dance Ensemble (page 64), are always worked counter-clockwise around the motif unless otherwise specified in the pattern.

SPECIAL TECHNIQUES

Most of the techniques used in the patterns can be found in a basic how-to-crochet book. I often recommend *Teach Yourself Visually: Crochet* by Kim Werker and Cecily Keim because it has clear illustrations and easy-to-understand explanations of basic techniques. This book is a great resource for crochet work like seaming, joining, and other finishing techniques. If you're a new crocheter you'll find most of the patterns in *Crochet for Bears to Wear* accessible, but you may want to have a basic crochet reference handy. You'll find some special stitch patterns at the beginning of certain pattern instructions, and I've included a complete list of common abbreviations on page 92.

This section gives instructions for the techniques and stitches most frequently used in the patterns—and those that may not be found in a basic how-to-crochet book.

WORKING IN THE ROUND USING THE BASIC HAT TECHNIQUE

Many of the patterns in this book are crocheted in the round and use the Basic Hat Technique as a starting point. You'll work this pattern in the round using the Adjustable Ring method (page 12), and you will require stitch markers to mark your increases. This pattern is worked in spiraled rounds without turns or joins after the first round.

Begin with an Adjustable Ring (page 12).

Round 1 *Work 6 sc into the center of the ring, sl st in first sc to join (6 stitches). Do not turn.*

Round 2 *Work 2 sc in each sc of the previous round (12 stitches). Place markers in every other stitch to indicate where increases will be made.*

Round 3 (Inc) **Sc in each stitch to marked stitch, 2 sc in marked stitch (increase made), and move this marker to second stitch just made; repeat from * around (18 stitches).*

Repeat Round 3 until the crown of your hat reaches just shy of the circumference of the head you're trying to fit. (The crown will grow slightly even after you stop increasing).

Work even in single crochet until the sides of the hat are the right length for your toy's head. Fasten off.

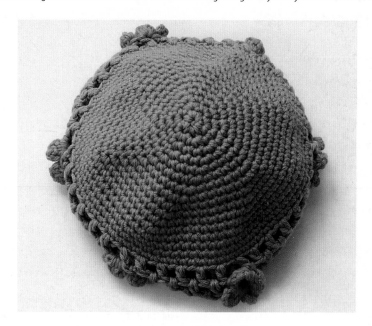

Working in the Round

One of the most common techniques in crochet is working in the round. For crocheting in the round, the fabric can either be joined at the ends of rounds with a slip stitch, or the stitches can be worked in a spiral without joins so that there's no obvious beginning or end to the round. Spiraled rounds are most often worked in single crochet, as it becomes awkward to spiral with taller stitches. When rounds are joined, they can be turned as with rows, turning and working on the wrong side of the work every other row, or they can be joined without turning to create a two-sided fabric.

There are a few methods to begin working in the round. If no method is specified in a pattern, feel free to choose the one you like best.

Method 1

Adjustable Ring: Holding the yarn end with your thumb and index finger, wrap the yarn twice clockwise around your fingers to make a ring. Pinch the ring and the tail to hold the ring together. Insert the hook into the center of the ring and pull up a loop; chain one to secure.

Round 1 Work the specified number of stitches into the ring, inserting the hook through the ring to make each stitch. Join with a slip stitch to the first stitch to complete your first round. Pull gently on the tail of your ring to close the center. (The center might loosen as you work, but will stay closed once you weave in your ends).

Method 2

Chain Ring: To begin crocheting in the round with a chain, simply chain the number of stitches specified (usually 4 or 6), and then join the first chain to the last with a slip stitch to form a ring. Work the next round of stitches into the center of the chain ring.

Method 3

Chain-2 (Ch-2) Start: Another way to begin a circular motif is with a Ch-2. Ch 2, then work the specified number of stitches (probably 4, 6, or 8) into the second chain from the hook. Join the last stitch to the first with a slip stitch to form your first round.

Changing Colors in Crochet

When working a project that requires two colors, simply pick up the new color and start crocheting with it into the last stitch of the previous color when changing colors at the end of a row. By working the final yarn over of the previous colored stitch in the new color, the entire next stitch will be worked in the new color.

In the Fair Isle Sweater (page 78) the unused colors are carried on the wrong side of the work, floating behind the stitches in the traditional Fair Isle fashion. But crocheted colorwork can also be worked by laying the unused color across the stitches of the row below and working over them. This creates a stiffer fabric that is great for hats, bags, or baskets.

Working in the Front or Back Loop

If you look down from the top at a row of crocheted stitches, you'll see a line of sideways "Vs." These "Vs" are made up of two loops called the front loop (the one closest to you when you're crocheting) and the back loop (the one farthest from you when you're crocheting). Most of the time, your crochet hook passes under both of these loops to form a stitch, but sometimes a pattern stitch will call for you to work in the front loop only (flo) or the back loop only (blo). Using these different loops can create a variety of interesting crochet textures. Crocheted ribbing, for instance, is the most common use of back-loop crochet. To create the ribbing, each stitch of each row is worked in the back loop.

Post Stitches

To create the cabled texture used in the Fisherman's Sweater (page 88), designer Drew Emborsky uses post stitches. Instead of working the stitch in the usual place, post stitches are worked around the "post" or the vertical line of the stitch from the row below.

Front Post Double Crochet (fpdc): Yarn over, from the front of the work, insert the hook from right to left around the post of the next stitch from the row below, yarn over, and pull up a loop. Then complete the double crochet as usual.

Back Post Double Crochet (bpdc): Yarn over, from the back of the work, insert the hook from right to left around the post of the next stitch from the row below, yarn over, and pull up a loop. Then complete the double crochet as usual.

Extended Single Crochet (esc)

As the name suggests, an extended single crochet stitch is taller than single crochet. To form an extended single crochet stitch, insert the hook into the next stitch or space indicated, pull up a loop, yarn over, pull through one loop on hook, yarn over, and pull through both loops on hook.

Foundation Single Crochet (fsc)

Foundation single crochet is a method for beginning your project with a row of single crochet stitches instead of a foundation chain. It's helpful when you want a foundation that's just as stretchy at the start as it is at the final row, or for situations where you're going to be crocheting into both sides of your foundation.

To work foundation single crochet, chain 2, insert the hook into the second chain from the hook, yarn over, pull up a loop, chain 1, yarn over, and pull through both loops on the hook. The next stitch is worked into the extra chain you just made. *Insert the hook into the chain-1 you just made, yarn over, pull up a loop, chain 1, yarn over, and pull through both loops on the hook.** Repeat from * to ** to create the length of foundation needed.

Linked Double Crochet (ldc)

Linked double crochet creates a solid fabric by joining stitches in the center as well as the top of the stitch. Chain 3, insert the hook into the second chain of the chain-3 just made, pull up a loop, skip the first stitch (or work into the fourth chain from the hook if you're working into a foundation chain), insert the hook into the next stitch, pull up a loop, yarn over, pull through 2 loops, yarn over, pull through 2 loops, *insert the hook into middle horizontal "bar" of the double crochet just made, pull up a loop, insert the hook into the next stitch, pull up a loop, yarn over, pull through 2 loops, yarn over, and pull through 2 loops.** Repeat from * to ** for each linked double crochet.

TOOLS

A bit of yarn and a hook are the only absolute necessities for crochet, but there are many options from which to choose. A few additional tools will make stitching easier and more efficient.

Hooks: Most crochet hooks cost just a few dollars, making them one of the least expensive tools in the crocheter's tool box. It's easy to establish a large collection of hooks, and you'll want to have a wide variety sizes on hand. (I often find old hook sets at estate and garage sales.) Hooks are small, so you can keep several in your project bag should you ever need to change sizes.

Crochet hooks have a complicated naming scheme. The tiniest steel hooks used for thread crochet are numbered, and the higher the number, the smaller the hook. These numbers correspond with numbers assigned to the weight of the thread used with the hook. Beyond the steel hooks, in the United States, hooks are sized by the letters B–S, with B being the smallest and S being the largest. Those lettered hooks are also sometimes assigned numbers to correspond with their complementary knitting needles (i.e., a size H hook is the same diameter as a size 8 knitting needle). The only truly empirical way of measuring hooks is by diameter, which is measured in millimeters. For instance, a size H/8 hook is 5mm. I will use all three (U.S. H/8/5mm) when describing hooks. You'll find a comprehensive chart of hook sizes on page 93.

In addition to the myriad sizes, there are two distinct styles of crochet hook: Boye and Bates. Yes, these are also hook brand names, but if you compare the two you'll see that the shape of the hook itself and the way the shaft is tapered are different. Most hook manufacturers adopt one or the other style.

Hooks also come in many different materials. I prefer to work with nickel-plated aluminum hooks because they are fast and lightweight and their plastic handles are comfortable to hold. I also like to use bamboo hooks and handmade hardwood hooks, as some kinds of yarn seem to "feel" better with a certain hook material. Silk yarn can be too slippery for nickel-plated aluminum, and wool yarn sometimes feels slow on bamboo. Choosing your hook is a question of trial and error and knowing what you like.

Yarn: When choosing yarn for crochet I consider a number of things. I ask myself questions about the drape and hand (softness) of the yarn, how the yarn will show the stitch pattern, whether the color fits the project, and—when crocheting for children—whether the yarn is machine-washable. Some of these questions are subjective—do I like the way a particular yarn feels, for example. For me, natural fibers feel best and, because I'm concerned about the impact that my crafting has on the world around me, I do my best to work with yarn companies that make environmental sustainability and social equality a foundation of their business.

Other answers to my questions can be found using measurable data. Yarn weight can be a great predictor of how a yarn will behave in a finished garment. For the most part, I tend to crochet with sportweight or DK-weight yarn, and sometimes even lighter yarns. Occasionally, I'll use worsted or chunky yarns, but only if I specifically want a big-stitch look, a stiff fabric, or a warm project. Sometimes a bulkier yarn can be used to good effect with a lacy or openwork stitch pattern. When there's a lot of air between stitches, bulky yarns can produce a nice drape. In general, however, sportweight and DK yarns make it easier to get a flowing fabric with crochet stitches. They also help to ensure that the finished garment is not too heavy.

The easiest way to substitute yarns for those shown in the projects is to choose one that gives you the same gauge. When I'm trying to match gauge, I look at the weight per skein and the number of yards or meters given in the pattern materials and compare it to the yarn I wish to substitute. The Craft Yarn Council has developed guidelines for classifying weights of yarn, which may be useful for making substitutions (page 93). Because the customizing sidebars use measurements, you can make projects to the size needed for your bear or toy using a yarn that yields a different gauge. Be careful using very bulky yarns for tiny bear projects. You'll find that a stitch or two can add an inch (2.5 cm), or more to your project, and therefore accurate gauge and careful calculations become even more important.

Measuring Tape: I prefer to use a flexible dressmaker's measuring tape, the kind that retracts at the touch of a button. Some hook and needle gauges come with a ruler that makes it easy to measure gauge swatches.

Yarn Needle: A yarn needle looks like an oversized sewing needle, with a large eye for ease of threading and a blunt tip so it won't snag the yarn. Some yarn needles have bent tips that make it easy to dig in and around stitches for weaving in ends or seaming together pieces of garments.

Removable Stitch Markers: A few of the projects in the book call for stitch markers. You can buy coil-less safety pins or use standard safety pins, but the latter sometimes catch on the yarn. Loops made from waste yarn also work well, or you can do as I sometimes do and bend a plastic-coated paper clip into a ring to use as a marker. If you're buying stitch markers at a yarn store, be sure they're removable, and are not the closed ring style often used for knitting.

Pins: Pins can be useful for blocking your work or for pinning pieces before assembly. Choose rust-proof pins if possible. T or U-shaped pins work well for blocking since they don't fall through holes in your work, as standard sewing pins might.

Scissors: A quality pair of scissors is a worthwhile investment. In my house, everyone knows not to touch Mom's scissors. They're used only to cut yarn and therefore stay super-sharp and ready for the job.

Calculator: None of the calculations in the book are complicated, but if it helps, by all means use a calculator. I often do.

chapter 2

OUT OF *hibernation*

When the days get longer and the spring thaw begins,

our sleepy teddy bears stir out of hibernation. Joey knows that spring

can mean getting dirty, so he's ready for rough-and-tumble work and

play in his Spring Cleaning Jeans and T-Shirt (page 18). Always one

for action, he's ready to hit the bases during spring training in his 7th

Inning Stretch Baseball Jersey and Cap (page 24) and amigurumi-style

Bat and Ball (page 30). Spring is also a favorite time for Pearl, who

watches with keen anticipation as bees buzz around the blossoms that

will soon become her favorite berries. She loves to wear her Bear-y

Pickin' Dress and Bonnet (page 32) while hunting down orange-pink

salmonberries and elusive nagoon berries, the locations of which are

kept secret by the pickers in her native Alaska.

spring cleaning T-SHIRT AND JEANS

Joey's no fan of housework, but come springtime, he needs to dig his way out of hibernation and make room for more honey. He gets to work in a sturdy pair of dungarees and his favorite soft and comfy color–block T-shirt. Both are worked from the top down in one piece and have minimal finishing.

Skill Level
Easy

Finished Measurements

T-Shirt
KEY MEASUREMENT Neckband Circumference: 13" (33cm)

Chest Circumference: 17¼" (44cm)

Length: 4.5" (11.5cm)

Sleeve Length (from neck): 3" (7.5cm) including cuff

Neckband to Underarm Length: 3" (7.5cm)

Jeans
KEY MEASUREMENT Waistband, unstretched: 14" (35.5cm)

Inseam: 3½" (9cm)

Inseam Flap: 3" (7.5cm) wide

Leg Circumference: 9" (23cm)

Total Length: 6½" (16.5cm)

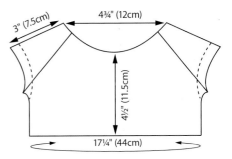

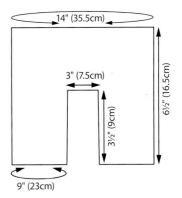

Materials

Stitch markers

Yarn needle

T-shirt

DMC-Senso Wool Cotton (70% cotton, 30% wool, 100yds [91m], 1oz [29 g]):
1 skein light moss green (A), 1 skein light tan (B), (**2**) fine

U.S. E/4 (3.5mm) crochet hook, or size needed to obtain gauge

Jeans

2 skeins DMC-Senso Denim (60% cotton, 40% acrylic; 150 yds [137m] per 1.5 oz [43g]), color: Dark Denim, (**2**) fine

U.S. H/8 (5mm) crochet hook, or size needed to obtain gauge

1 skein orange embroidery floss for optional embellishment

Tapestry needle for embroidery

Gauge

T-shirt

20 stitches and 16 rows = 4" (10cm) in alternating dc/sc pattern

Jeans

15 stitches and 15 rows = 4" (10cm) in sc-flo stitch using 2 strands of yarn (body)

SPRING CLEANING T-SHIRT

Ribbed Neckband

Ch 4.

Row 1 Sc in second chain from hook and in each chain across, turn—3 sc.

Row 2 Ch 1, sc-blo across, turn.

Repeat Row 2 for a total of 72 rows, (until the neckband measures 13" [33cm] unstretched). Fold the neckband in half so the foundation row is aligned with the final row. Place a marker to denote the start of the round. Sc the foundation to the final row to form a ring. Do not fasten off. Place a marker to denote the center back.

Body

Note: *In double crochet rounds, the turning chain does not count as a stitch and is not worked in the following round. The shirt is worked in joined rounds without turning.*

Round 1 Ch 1, sc around side edge of neckband, working 1 stitch for every row of the neckband, sl st in first sc to join—72 sc.

Round 2 Ch 3 (turning chain does not count as a stitch here and throughout), dc in each stitch around, sl st in the first dc to join.

Set Up Raglan Increases

Beginning at the center back, count 12 stitches and place marker, count 12 more stitches, place marker, count 24 stitches, place marker, count 12 stitches, place marker. Remove center back marker.

Begin Raglan Increases

Round 1 (**Inc**) Ch 1, *sc across to first marker, work 3 sc in marked stitch, and move marker to middle stitch of 3 sc just worked; repeat from * around, sc across to the end of the round, sl st in first sc to join—80 sc.

Round 2 Ch 3, dc in each stitch around, sl st in first dc to join.

Work Rounds 1–2 three more times or until the sleeve portion of the shirt almost fits around the bear's arm—104 dc. In the last stitch of the final round, change to color B.

Form Armholes

With color B, ch 1, sc across to the first marker, work 2 sc in the marked stitch, ch 9 (for underarm stitches), sl st in the next marked stitch, work 2 sc in the same stitch, sc to the next marker, work 2 sc in the marked stitch, ch 9, sl st in the next marked stitch, work 2 sc in the same stitch, sc to the end of the round, sl st in the first sc to join—68 sc and 18 ch.

T-Shirt Body

Round 1 With color B, ch 3, dc in each sc and ch st around, sl st in first dc to join—86 dc.

Round 2 Ch 1, sc evenly around, sl st in first sc to join.

Round 3 Ch 3, dc in each stitch around, sl st in first dc to join.

Repeat Rounds 2–3 once more, then repeat round 3 once again. In the last stitch of the final round, change to color A. Work one final sc round with color A. Fasten off.

Ribbed Cuffs

The cuffs are worked lengthwise, and joined to the sleeve as you go with two slip stitches per join. The first attaches the sides to the top; the second acts as the turning chain. With color A and RS facing, join yarn with a slip stitch to the edge of the sleeve at the underarm, ch 4.

Row 1 Sc in second chain from hook and in each chain across, sl st in the next 2 unworked stitches of the sleeve, turn—3 sc.

Row 2 Sc-blo in each sc across cuff, turn.

Row 3 Ch 1, sc-blo across to the sleeve edge, sl st in the next 2 unworked stitches of the sleeve, turn.

Repeat Rows 2–3 until the ribbing extends all the way around the sleeve. Sl st the edges of the ribbing together. Repeat for the second cuff.

Finishing

Weave in ends.

I I I I I I I I I I I I I I I I I I I I I I I I I I I I I I I I I I I I I I I I I I I I I I I I I I I I I I I I I I I

MAKE A CUSTOM-SIZED T-SHIRT

1. Begin with the ribbed neckband as written in the pattern. Work the neckband until it fits around your toy's neck unstretched. Count the rows. Adjust the row count to a multiple of 6 (adding rows is preferable to removing them unless you only need to remove one or two). Make a note of your final Row Count:

_____

2. When getting ready to set up for the raglan increases, divide the Row Count by 6:

(Row Count) ÷ 6 = _____ (N)

3. Beginning at center back, count (N) stitches and place marker, count (N) more stitches, place marker, count (Nx2) stitches, place marker, count (N) stitches, place marker.

4. Remove the center back marker. Follow the remainder of the pattern as written, adjusting the length of the T-shirt to fit your toy.

If you're crocheting for a toy very different in size from Joey, you'll also need to adjust the underarm stitches. Start with your stitch gauge (per inch/cm) and subtract 2:

Stitch gauge - 2 = _____(Underarm Stitches)

SPRING CLEANING JEANS

Note: *To make a sturdy denim-like fabric, the jeans are worked holding two strands of yarn together throughout the project. Jeans are worked in the round without joins or turns, with the exception of the inseam flap, which is worked back and forth in rows.*

Waistband

With 2 strands held together, ch 5.

Row 1 Sc in second chain and in each chain across, turn—4 sc.

Row 2 Ch 1, sc-blo across, turn.

Repeat Row 2 until the waistband measures 14" (35.5cm) unstretched. Fold the waistband in half so the foundation row is aligned with the final row. Working through both layers, sc the foundation to the final row to form a ring. Do not fasten off.

Body

Ch 1, sc around the side edge of the waistband, working 1 stitch for every row of the waistband. Place a marker to mark the center back and move up with each round. Do not turn. Sc-flo around evenly until jeans measure 2½" (6.5 cm) from the top of the waistband.

Inseam Flap

To set up the inseam flap, count the stitches and place a removable marker or safety pin directly across from the beginning of the round marker for the center front, dividing the stitches in half evenly.

Beginning at the center back marker, sc-flo in the next 5 stitches, place a marker in the stitch just worked, sc-flo to 4 stitches before the center front marker, place marker, sc-flo to 5 stitches after the center front at the center front marker, place marker. Remove the center front marker, sc-flo to 4 stitches before the center back marker, place marker, and remove the center back marker. There are 10 stitches marked at the center front and the center back, turn.

Row 1 (WS) Sc evenly over 10 stitches.

Row 2 (RS) Sc-flo across.

Repeat Rows 1–2 until the flap measures 3" (7.5cm).

With right sides together, sl st the final row of the flap to the marked 10 stitches at the center front of the jeans. Fasten off.

Leg

With right sides facing, join the yarn at the back corner of one leg where the inseam flap meets the body. Sc around the leg, working 1 stitch for every row edge of the Inseam Flap. Sc evenly around until the leg measures 3½" (9cm) from the inseam. Repeat for the second leg.

MAKE A CUSTOM-SIZED PAIR OF JEANS

1. Measure the hip length of your toy (waist to the beginning of inseam):

_____ *(Length)*

2. Measure the distance between your toy's legs:

_____ *(Width)*

3. Record stitch gauge (per inch/cm):

_____ *(Stitch Gauge)*

4. Multiply (Width) x (Stitch Gauge) and round to whole number:

_____ *(Inseam Flap Stitches)*

Begin the pattern as written, and work the waistband until it fits your toy when just slightly stretched. Work the body for (Length) and then set up for the inseam using (Inseam Flap Stitches) instead of the number called for in the pattern. Work the inseam flap until it reaches the center front of the body comfortably. Follow the remainder of the pattern, adjusting the length of the legs to fit your toy.

Finishing

Weave in ends. With orange embroidery floss and using a ⅛" (3mm) long running stitch, stitch around the body just below the waistband and stitch an arc over each leg for front pockets (see photo, opposite).

7th inning stretch BASEBALL JERSEY, CAP, BAT, AND BALL

Fresh out of hibernation, Joey is eager to get to spring training. In this ball cap and jersey, he's ready for opening day. The jersey is crocheted in modular style from the center out in soft, durable cotton yarn. The cap is constructed from four wedge-shaped pieces; the brim is added after these are sewn together. With such a stylish uniform, Joey just has to grab his trusty Bat and Ball (page 30), and is sure to win the title of Best–Dressed.

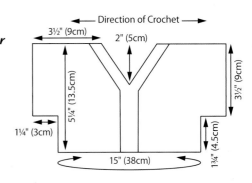

BASEBALL JERSEY AND CAP

Skill Level
Intermediate

Finished Measurements

Jersey
KEY MEASUREMENT Length (back neck to hem): 5¼" (13.5cm)

Chest circumference: 15" (38cm)

Armhole Depth: 3½" (9cm)

V-neck Depth: 2" (5cm)

Sleeve Length: 1¼" (3cm)

Cap
KEY MEASUREMENT Cap Circumference: 13" (33cm)

Width of pieces: 3¼" (8.25cm)

Length of pieces: 3½" (9cm)

Materials
Elmore Pisagh Peaches & Crème 4 Ply Worsted Weight (100% cotton; 122 yds [111.5m] per 2.5 oz [70.9g]):
2 skeins color #10 yellow (A), 2 skeins color #19 Peacock (B), (4) medium

U.S. H/8 (5mm) crochet hook or size needed to obtain gauge

Stitch markers

Yarn Needle

Gauge
8 stitches and 9 rows = 2" (5cm) in sc

Crown Piece

modular crochet

The 7th Inning Stretch Baseball Jersey uses a construction technique called modular crochet, which was developed in the 1970s by Judith Copeland. Modular crochet garments are constructed sideways in pieces from the center of the garment to the edges. Each piece is added directly onto the last piece worked, joining as you go, so there's minimal finishing. It's a great way to create custom-sized garments.

7TH INNING STRETCH BASEBALL JERSEY

V-neck Front

With color A, fsc 21, turn.

Row 1 (RS) Ch 1, sc across first 14 stitches, fsc 7 stitches to create second side of V-neck, turn—21 sc.

Left Front

Row 1 (WS) With color B, ch 1, sc across, turn.

Rows 2–6 Ch 1, sc across, turn. Fasten off.

Back and Right Front

With color B, fsc 21, turn.

Row 1 (RS) Ch 1, sc across, turn—21 sc.

Rows 2–6 Work as for Row 1, turn.

Row 7 Ch 1, sc across, sc in the first stitch at neck edge on Right Front (unworked side) of V-neck opening, sc across Front, turn—42 sc.

Rows 8–16 Ch 1, sc across front and back, turn.

Underarm Gusset

Row 1 Ch 1, sc across first 7 stitches, turn—7 sc.

Rows 2–5 Work as for Row 1. Fasten off.

Back and Left Front

With WS facing, join B to unworked side of back fsc at hem edge.

Row 1 Ch 1, sc across, turn—21 sc.

Rows 2–12 Work as for Row 1, turn.

Row 13 Ch 1, sc across back stitches, sc in first stitch of Left Front at neck edge with wrong sides facing, sc across, turn—42 sc.

Rows 14–16 Ch 1, sc across front and back stitches, turn.

Underarm Gusset

Work Underarm Gusset as for Right side. Fasten off.

Sleeves

With RS facing, join color A to Left Front 8 stitches from hem edge. Ch 1, sc across front, shoulder, and back until 8 stitches remain, turn. Work even across color A stitches only for 4 more rows. Repeat for second side.

Finishing

Fold garment in half at shoulders with RS together. Sew up sleeve and side seams. Weave in ends.

MAKE A CUSTOM-SIZED BASEBALL JERSEY

Note: *Round all calculations to the nearest whole number. Be sure row numbers for the left and right sides match.*

1. *Measure your toy's body length from neck to hip:* _____ *(Length)*

2. *Divide chest circumference ÷ 2:* _____ *(Front Width)*

3. *Record stitch gauge (per inch/cm):* _____ *(Stitch Gauge)*

4. *Record row gauge (per inch/cm):* _____ *(Row Gauge)*

5. *Multiply (Stitch Gauge) x (Length):* _____ *(Foundation Single Crochet)*

6. *Calculate stitches for V-neck: (Foundation Single Crochet) ÷ 3 =* _____ *(V-neck Stitches)*

7. *Calculate rows needed for Right/Left Front: (Row Gauge) x [(Front Width) ÷ 2] =* _____ *(Front Rows)*

8. *Calculate Underarm Gusset stitches: (Foundation Single Crochet) x .33 =* _____ *(Gusset Stitches)*

9. *Calculate gusset rows: [(Front Rows) ÷ 3] + 1 =* _____ *(Gusset Rows)*

10. *Calculate sleeve rows: (Front Rows) ÷ 2 =* _____ *(Sleeve Rows)*

Work the (Foundation Single Crochet) stitches. Following the pattern instructions, divide for the V-neck using (V-neck Stitches). Work Left Front as written in the pattern using (Front Rows) less 4–5 rows, to create the neck opening. Create Back using the same (Foundation Single Crochet) and work Back and Right Fronts according to pattern instructions, making sure you've worked enough rows to cover the width of your bear's shoulder. Work Underarm Gusset using (Gusset Stitches) and (Gusset Rows). Work second side of back and the remainder of left front according to the pattern, being sure the number of rows worked left matches the number worked right. Work the second Underarm Gusset as for the first. Begin Sleeves in stitch above (Gusset Stitches) and work to the other side, leaving equal stitches remaining at the opposite edge. Work length according to (Sleeve Rows). Finish according to pattern instructions.

| | | | | | | | | | | | | | | | | | | | | | | | | | | | | | | | | | | | | | | | | | | | | | | | | | | | | | | | | | | | | | | | | | | | | | | | | | |

Crown Pieces

(make 2 with A and 2 with B)

Ch 3.

Row 1 (Inc) 2 sc in second chain from hook and remaining chain, turn—4 sc.

Row 2 (Inc) Ch 1, 2 sc in first stitch, sc across, turn—5 sc.

Work as for Row 2 until you have 13 stitches. Work even for 1" (2.5cm) from crown. Fasten off.

Assembly

Place two color A triangles with wrong sides facing each other and sl st one side together for the back. Repeat with color B triangles for the front. Place the two halves together with wrong sides together and sl st closed, center 6 stitches at the crown of the hat and 3 stitches on both sides of the bottom of the hat. Leave the remaining stitches unworked as ear openings. Seams will show on the right side of the hat.

MAKE A CUSTOM-SIZED CAP

Note: *Round all calculations to the nearest whole number.*

1. Measure your toy's head (not including the ears):

_____ *(Head Circumference)*

2. Divide (Head Circumference) ÷ 4:

_____ *(Crown Piece Width)*

3. Record stitch gauge (per inch/cm):

_____ *(Gauge)*

4. Calculate piece width: (Gauge) x (Crown Piece Width) =

_____ *(Total Stitches)*

Begin the pattern as written, working increase rows until the stitch count matches (Total Stitches). Work even for 1" (2.5cm) or just about ½" (13mm) if your toy is very small. Follow the pattern for cap assembly, adjusting the size of the ear openings as necessary. Work the brim and button according to the pattern, adjusting the length of the brim as necessary for your toy.

Brim

With WS of the cap's front facing, join A at one side seam under the ear, sl st across the front of the hat to the opposite side seam, turn—26 stitches.

Row 1 Ch 1, sc to 1 stitch before center seam of front, work 2 sc in next 2 stitches, placing two markers in the 2 center stitches, sc across, turn—28 sc.

Row 2 Ch 1, sc2tog, sc across to markers work 2 sc in each marked stitch, remove markers, sc across, turn—29 sc.

Row 3 Ch 1, sc2tog, sc across, turn—28 sc.

Rows 4–8 Repeat Row 3—23 sc.

Row 9 Sl st into 1st stitch, sc across, sl st into last stitch. Fasten off.

Brim Edging

With right sides facing, join B at the side seam under the ear, and sl st evenly across brim to the opposite seam. Fasten off. Weave in ends.

Button

With color A, begin with an Adjustable Ring (page 12).

Work 6 sc into the ring, sl st in first sc to join, pull tail to close the ring. Fasten off. Use tails to sew the button to the top of the hat.

Joey is always up for playing ball or attending a game, and his favorite bat and ball are just the right size for teddy paws. Made in classic amigurumi crocheted toy style, this pair is sure to delight both little hands and little paws.

Skill Level

Easy

Finished Measurements

Bat
Height: 8" (20.5cm)
Circumference at widest point: 9" (23cm)

Ball
Circumference: 6" (15cm)

Materials

U.S. H/8 (5mm) crochet hook, or size needed to obtain gauge

Stitch markers

Small amount of fiberfill stuffing or wool roving

Yarn needle

Bat
1 ball Elmore-Pisgah Peaches and Crème (100% cotton, 122yds [111.5m], 2.5 oz [70g]), color: #92, Army Tan (B), (4) medium

Ball
1 ball Elmore-Pisgah Peaches and Crème (100% cotton, 122yds [111.5m], 2.5 oz [70g]), color: #5, Eggshell (A), (4) medium

1 skein orange embroidery thread

2.5mm steel crochet hook for baseball stitching

Fabric glue

Pencil

Gauge

16 stitches and 16 rows = 4" (10cm) in sc in the round

BAT

With larger hook and color B, work in single crochet the first 6 rounds as for Basic Hat Technique (page 11)—36 sc.

Work even for 5 rounds. Place a marker in every twelfth stitch (3 markers). Begin decreases:

Round 1 *Sc to one stitch before marked stitch, sc2tog moving marker up to new stitch; repeat from * around (33 sc).

Rounds 2–3 Sc in each stitch around moving marker up with each round.

Repeat Rounds 1–3 until 15 stitches remain. Work even for 2 more rounds.

Increase for handle end: Work [sc in next stitch, 2 sc in next stitch] around until you have 22 stitches. Work one round even. Work 1 round sc-flo.

Decrease for handle end: Work [sc in next stitch, sc2tog] around until 6 stitches remain. Stuff bat with stuffing until firm. Weave tail through remaining stitches and pull to draw remaining hole closed. Weave in ends.

BALL

With larger hook and color A, work in single crochet first 4 rounds as for Basic Hat Technique (page 11)—24 sc. Work 3 rounds even.

Begin decreases: Place marker in every fourth stitch (6 markers). *Sc around to one stitch before the marked stitch, sc2tog, moving marker to new stitch; repeat from * around—18 sc. Repeat the decrease round until 6 sc remain. Fasten off. Stuff the ball with stuffing. Weave the tail through the remaining stitches and pull to draw remaining hole closed. Weave in ends.

Finishing

To create baseball stitching, use the photo as a guide to draw a pencil line of stitching lightly onto the ball. Using the embroidery thread and smaller hook, crochet a chain long enough to cover the pencil-drawn line. Apply fabric glue to the pencil line and glue the chain to the baseball. Allow glue to dry fully and then hide ends of chain inside the ball.

amigurumi

Amigurumi simply means knit or crocheted doll. The word originated in Japan, where the making of amigurumi is wildly popular. Amigurumi are created using the Adjustable Ring Technique (page 12) with tight single crochet stitches worked in the round. When crocheting dolls, you can work on the arms and legs as you go or make them separately and sew them on later. The possibilities for embellishment—embroidery, sewn eyes, appliqué—are endless. The 7th Inning Stretch Bat and Ball projects are a simple introduction to the amigurumi style. Using this technique, you'll be able to vary your increases and decreases to create a bat and ball best suited for your little slugger.

bear-y pickin' DRESS AND BONNET

Raspberries, blueberries, strawberries—any berry will do for Pearl, a berry-picking expert. She loves to wear her delicate salmonberry-colored dress in or out of the berry bush. This lacy knee-length tunic has a ribbed top, which is worked from side to side. The sleeves and skirt are picked up and worked down from the top so there's no seaming. Of course, Pearl's berry-picking ensemble wouldn't be complete without a salmonberry-flowered cloche to keep her ears safe from prickly bushes. The Basic Hat Technique (page 11), creates the crown, and a double-crocheted mesh shows off the tiny flower embellishment, worked right onto the fabric.

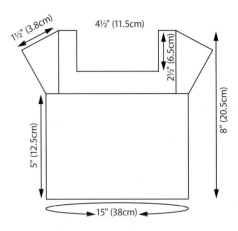

Skill Level

Dress
Intermediate

Bonnet
Easy

Finished Measurements

Dress
KEY MEASUREMENT Armhole Depth: 3½" (9cm)

Chest Circumference: 15" (38cm)

Length (back neck to hem): 8" (20.5cm)

Cap Sleeve (shoulder to cuff): 1½" (3.8cm)

Neck Width: 4½" (11.5cm)

U-neck Depth: 2½" (6cm)

Length of lace skirt: 5" (12.5cm) including border

Bonnet
KEY MEASUREMENT Hat Circumference: 17" (43cm)

Length (crown to brim): 4 ½" (11.5cm)

Materials

Brown Sheep Cotton Fleece (80% cotton, 20% merino wool, 215yds [197m], 3.5 oz [100g]): 1 skein terracotta canyon (A), 1 skein lime light (B), (❸) light

U.S. H/8 (5mm) crochet hook, or size needed to obtain gauge

Stitch markers

Yarn needle

Gauge

Dress
8 stitches and 7 rows = 2" (5cm) in sc-blo

Bonnet
8½ stitches and 9 rows = 2" (5cm) in sc

Special Stitches

V-stitch (v-st) Work 2 dc in the stitch or space indicated.

Shell (shell) Work 5 dc in the stitch or space indicated.

V-space (v-sp) The space in between the 2 dc that make up a v-stitch.

BEAR-Y PICKIN' DRESS

Left Shoulder

With color A, ch 21.

Row 1 (WS) Sc in second chain from hook and each chain across, turn—20 sc.

Row 2 Ch 1, sc-blo across, turn.

Rows 3–7 Repeat Row 2. Do not fasten off.

Back

Row 1 (RS) Ch 1, sc-blo in first 9 stitches, turn leaving remaining stitches unworked—9 stitches.

Rows 2–16 Work even in sc on 9 stitches. Do not fasten off.

armhole. Turn to work across front, sc evenly along row ends across left front shoulder, ch 8 to form the front neck, sc evenly along the row ends across right front shoulder, ch 7, sl st in first stitch of right back shoulder to form the right armhole. Place a marker for beginning of row—51 stitches.

Waistband

Work one round of sc in each stitch and ch around without joining or turning. In the last stitch of the round, change to color B. Work 2 rounds of sc in color B, then change back to color A and work one final round of sc in color A and working 2 sts in the last st, increase the stitch count to be an even number—52 stitches.

Right Shoulder

Row 1 (RS) Ch 1, sc-blo across, ch 12, turn.
Row 2 Sc in second chain from hook and in each chain across, sc-blo across back, turn—20 sc.
Row 3 Ch 1, sc-blo across, turn.
Rows 4–8 Repeat Row 2. Do not fasten off.

Armholes

Turn to work across long edge of back, sc in the end of every other row across the side of the work to the foundation edge. Fold the top in half lengthwise, so side edges are aligned. Ch 7, sl st in first stitch at the opposite end of the row to form the left

Lace Skirt

Note: *Worked in joined rounds without turning.*
Round 1 Ch 3 (counts as first dc here and throughout), dc in first stitch, *sk 1 stitch, v-st in next stitch; repeat from * around, end sk 1 stitch, sl st to top of beginning ch-3 to join (52 stitches).
Round 2 Ch 3, dc in first stitch, *v-st in first stitch of v-stitch from row below; repeat from * around, sl st to top of beginning ch-3 to join. Repeat Round 2 until skirt measures 4.5" (11.5cm).

Shell Edging

Ch 3, work 4 dc in first stitch, sk 2 stitches, *sc in next stitch, sk 1 stitch, shell in next stitch, sk

1 stitch; repeat from * around, ending with sc in last stitch, sl st in top of beginning ch-3 to join. Fasten off.

Sleeves

With right sides facing, join color B to underarm of first sleeve. Ch 1, sc in each stitch around, increasing stitch count to an even number if necessary—26 stitches.
Round 1 Ch 3, dc in first stitch, *sk 1 stitch, v-st in next stitch; repeat from * around, end sk 1 stitch, sl st in top of beginning ch-3 to join.
Round 2 Ch 3, dc in first v-sp, v-st in next and in each v-sp around, sl st in top of beginning chain-3 to join.
Repeat Round 2 once more. Fasten off.
Repeat for second Sleeve.

Finishing

Weave in ends.

BEAR-Y PICKIN' BONNET

Note: *Pearl's hat is meant to fit over her ears, but you can make your bonnet to sit on your bear's head just the way you'd like.*

With color B, begin as for Basic Hat Technique (page 11) until you have 74 sc, or the crown is the correct size for your bear. Work 4 rounds even in sc.

Mesh Sides

Round 1 Ch 4 (counts as dc, ch 1), sk the first

MAKE A CUSTOM-SIZED BEAR-Y PICKIN' DRESS

1. Measure your toy from the shoulder to the center back (do not include the distance across the underarm):

_____ *(Armhole Depth)*

2. Record stitch gauge (per inch/cm):

_____ *(Gauge)*

3. Multiply (Gauge) x (Armhole Depth):

_____ *(Total Stitches)*

4. Calculate foundation chain: (Total Stitches) + 1 =

_____ *(Foundation Chain)*

5. Calculate Back stitches: [(Total Stitches) ÷ 2] – 1 =

_____ *(Back Stitches)*

6. Calculate underarm chain: [(Gauge) x 2)] -1 =

_____ *(Underarm Chain)*

7. Calculate front neck: Rows on the back between shoulders ÷ 2 =

_____ *(Front Neck Rows)*

Work the (Foundation Chain) according to your calculations, and then work the first shoulder according to the pattern until your shoulder is the width of your toy's shoulder. Create the back using (Back Stitches) and working the length of your toy's back to the next shoulder. Work the second shoulder to match the first. Create the armholes using (Underarm Chain). Use the (Front Neck Rows) to join the bodice all the way around. Follow the rest of the pattern as written, adjusting the length of the skirt for your toy.

2 stitches, dc in next stitch, *ch 1, sk 1 stitch, dc in next stitch; repeat from * around, end with ch 1, sl st to third chain of beginning chain-4 to join—37 mesh spaces.

Round 2 Sl st to ch-1 sp, ch 4 (counts as dc, ch1), *sk next dc, dc in next ch-sp, ch1; repeat from * around, sl st in third chain of beginning ch-4 to join. Repeat Round 2. Fasten off.

Salmonberry Flowers

The flowers are worked around the stitches that surround the holes in the mesh.

Petal 1 With color A, join yarn with sl st to a dc post in Round 2 of mesh at the center front of the hat. Ch 3, work 2 dc around the post of the same stitch, sl st around the same stitch, turn work clockwise.

Petal 2 Sl st into the ch-sp now facing you, ch 3, 2 dc around the ch-sp, sl st in the same space, turn work clockwise.

Petal 3 Work as for Petal 1 around dc that's opposite Petal 1.

Petal 4 Work as for Petal 2 in the ch-sp opposite Petal 2. Sl st to join the round. Fasten off.

Work Salmonberry Flowers approximately every 7 mesh spaces evenly around the hat.

Finishing

Weave in ends.

chapter 3

HEAT *wave*

Long hot days call for fun in the sun; whether on cool, sandy beaches or by clear mountain streams, this furry threesome likes to chill out when the temperature rises. Eddie and Pearl head straight for the surf. Eddie loves to seek out the perfect wave: When he hangs "paw," you'll find him dressed in his Endless Summer Board Shorts (page 38). Pearl watches from her perch on the sand, looking her best (as always) in her California Dreamin' Bikini (page 42). Meanwhile, Joey heads upstream in his Gone Fishing Vest (page 46), eager to catch some salmon on their way to spawn.

endless summer BOARD SHORTS

When the weather's right, you'll find Eddie at the beach. Whether riding the waves or simply fishing for a snack, he's ready for the water in these cheery board shorts. An integrated ribbed waistband and internal drawstring allow them to sit low on the hips. Because they're crocheted sideways in one piece, there's minimal finishing, meaning you'll be at the beach in no time.

Skill Level
Easy

Finished Measurements
KEY MEASUREMENT Length: 4" (10cm)
Width circumference: 18" (45.5cm)
Inseam: 1¾" (4.5cm)

Materials
Classic Elite Cotton Bam Boo (52% cotton, 48% bamboo, 130 yds [119m], 1.75 oz [50g]):
1 skein #3648, Heron Blue (A), 1 skein #3685, Tiger Lily (B), light

U.S. E/4 (3.5mm) crochet hook, or size needed to obtain gauge

Stitch markers

Yarn needle

Gauge
10 stitches and 14 rows = 2" (5cm) in sc

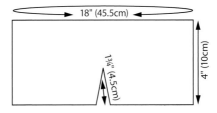

Left Leg

Using color A, ch 21.

Row 1 (WS) Sc in second chain from hook and in each chain across, turn—20 sc.

Row 2 Ch 1, sc-blo in first 5 stitches (forms waistband), sc across, turn.

Row 3 Ch 1, sc across to last 5 stitches, sc-blo to end, turn.

Repeat Rows 2–3 for a total of 25 rows from beginning, ending with Row 3.

Front Inseam

Row 1 (RS) Ch 1, sc-blo in first 5 stitches, sc across next 6 stitches, ch 10, turn—11 sc.

Row 2 Sc in 2nd ch from hook, sc in each ch and st across to last 5 stitches, sc-blo to end, turn—20 sc.

Right Leg

Repeat Rows 2–3 of left leg for a total of 25 rows from inseam for right front leg.

Change to color B, continue in pattern for 12 rows for right side. Change to color A, work 25 rows in pattern for right back leg, and then create back inseam as for front. Work 25 rows in pattern with color A for left back leg, change to color B, continue in pattern for 12 rows for left side. Fasten off.

Finishing

With right sides together, sew side seam and inseams. Weave in ends.

Do not turn right side out.

Belt Loop

Mark the center front. Join color A 2 stitches from row edge at center back and ch 3; skip the next 2 stitches of same row and sl st into the next stitch. Fasten off.

Work one belt loop every tenth row around waistband except at the center front where you will make 2 belt loops 2 rows apart, placing one on each side of the center front. Work belt loops in color B over color B rows. Turn right side out.

Drawstring

Using color B, ch 131, sc in second chain and in each chain across, turn—130 sc. Ch 1, sc across, fasten off.

Weave in ends.

Thread the drawstring through the belt loops and tie the ends together at the front.

CREATE A CUSTOM-SIZED PAIR OF BOARD SHORTS

1. Measure your bear's waist at the widest point (on Eddie, this is his hips, not his waist) _____ (Waist)

2. Measure from the waist down to where you'd like the shorts to fall: _____ (Length)

3. Record stitch gauge (per inch/cm): _____ (Stitch Gauge)

4. Record row gauge (per inch/cm): _____ (Row Gauge)

5. Multiply [(Length) x (Stitch Gauge)]: _____ (Stitches per Row)

6. Add (Stitches per Row) + 1: _____ (Foundation Chain)

7. Multiply (Waist) x (Row Gauge): _____ (Total Rows rounded to whole number)

8. Calculate Inseam: [(Stitches per Row) x .45] + 1 = _____ (Inseam Foundation Chain)

9. Calculate ribbed stitches: (Stitches per Row) x .25 = _____ (Ribbed Stitches)

10. Subtract (Inseam Foundation Chain) and (Ribbed Stitches) from (Stitches per Row):

_____ (stitches worked before Inseam)

11. (Total Rows) x .2 = _____ (Right Front/Left Front rounded to whole number)

12. (Total Rows) x .1 = _____ (Color B Side Rows rounded to whole number)

Begin with color A and your calculated (Foundation Chain). Work according to the pattern, substituting your calculations for the row counts and stitch counts indicated in the pattern. Create a drawstring 1½ times the circumference of the waistband.

California dreamin' BIKINI

Pearl prefers relaxing in the sun with a cool glass of lemonade to playing in the waves, and she does so in style in her striped bikini. The variegated cotton stretch yarn creates a delightful shaded stripe pattern. Since each piece is a simple rectangle worked in ribbed stitch with minimal finishing, this bikini makes a great beginner project.

Skill Level
Easy

Finished Measurements
KEY MEASUREMENT Length (waistband to bottom of leg opening): 4½" (11.5cm)

Top Width: 5" (12.5cm)

Top Height: 3¼" (8.5cm)

Waist: 12" (30.5cm), unstretched before waistband is added

Materials
1 ball Cascade Fixation (98.3% cotton, 1.7% elastic, 100 yards [91.4m], 1.75oz [50g]), color: #9245, ( ) light

U.S. D/3 (3.25mm) crochet hook, or size needed to obtain gauge

Yarn needle

Gauge
22 stitches and 39 rows = 4" (10cm) in sc-blo

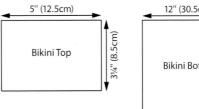

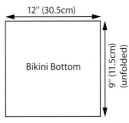

Bikini Top — 5" (12.5cm) × 3¼" (8.5cm)

Bikini Bottom — 12" (30.5cm) × 9" (11.5cm) (unfolded)

Ch 19.

Row 1 Sc in second chain from hook and in each chain across, turn—18 sc.

Row 2 Ch 1, sc-blo across, turn.

Repeat Row 2 until piece measures 5" (12.5 cm) from foundation. Fasten off. Weave in ends.

Ties (make 4)

Make a chain 13" (33 cm) long. Fasten off. Sew one chain to each corner of the Bikini Top.

MAKE A CUSTOM-SIZED BIKINI TOP

1. Measure your toy's chest between the arm joints: _____ *(Chest)*

2. Measure the distance between the shoulder and underarm: _____ *(Arm Height)*

3. Record the stitch gauge (per inch/cm): _____ *(Gauge)*

4. Multiply [(Gauge) x (Arm Height)] + 1: _____ *(Foundation Chain)*

Make sure to round your (Foundation Chain) up to a whole number. Using your rounded calculation for (Foundation Chain), follow the pattern as written, working even in sc-blo until the rectangle matches your (Chest) measurement. For each tie, multiply: 4 x (Arm Height).

Bikini Bottom

Ch 54.

Row 1 Sc in second chain from hook and in each chain across, turn—53 sc.

Row 2 Ch 1, sc-blo across, turn.

Repeat Row 2 until piece measures 6" (15.2cm) from foundation unstretched. Fasten off.

Assembly

Fold work in half so that the row-edges become the waistband. Sew the first 4 stitches of foundation row and final row together on either side at waist, leaving the remaining stitches open, to form side seams and leg holes.

Waistband

Join yarn at one seam of the waist opening. Sc around the row edges, placing one sc for every row. Work two more rounds sc.

Fasten off.

Weave in ends.

|||||||||||||||||||||||||||||||||||||||||||||||||||||||||||||||||

MAKE A CUSTOM-SIZED BIKINI BOTTOM

1. Measure around your toy's leg:

_____ *(Leg)*

2. Record stitch gauge (per inch/cm):

_____ *(Gauge)*

3. Calculate your foundation chain: ([(Leg) x (Gauge)] + [Gauge]) + 1 =

_____ *(Foundation Chain)*

Using your calculations for the (Foundation Chain), follow the instructions for the Bikini Bottom.

gone fishing VEST

Joey is always up for adventure, and fishing—whether with paw or rod—is one of his favorite summer activities. This soy-wool vest, worked in smooth granite stitch, keeps him cool, while handy patch pockets hold snacks and gear.

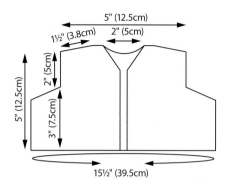

Skill Level
Intermediate

Finished Measurements
KEY MEASUREMENT Vest Circumference: 15½" (39.5cm)

Length: 5" (12.5cm)

Armhole Depth: 2" (5cm)

Back width: 5" (12.5cm)

Neck Width: 2" (5cm)

Shoulder: 1½" (3.8cm)

Foundation edge to underarm: 3" (7.5cm)

Materials
1 skein Southwest Trading Company Karaoke (50% Soy Silk, 50% Wool; 109 yds [100m]/1.75 oz [50g]), color:
#282 forest, (**3**) light

U.S. G/6 (4mm) crochet hook, or size needed to obtain gauge

Pipe cleaner, pony bead, and a bit of novelty yarn or roving for tiny fly lure (optional)

Measuring tape

Yarn needle

Gauge
16 stitches and 22 rows = 4" (10cm) in granite stitch

Special Stitches

Granite Stitch

Row 1 Ch 2, sk first stitch, sc in next stitch, *ch 1, sk 1 stitch, sc in next stitch; repeat from * across, turn.

Row 2 Ch 2, sk first sc, sc in next ch-1 sp, *ch 1, sk 1 st, sc in next ch-1 sp; repeat from * across, ending sc in ch-2 sp at end of row, turn.

Repeat Row 2 for pattern.

Ch 63.

Row 1 Sc in second chain from hook, sc in each chain across, turn—62 stitches. Work even in granite stitch pattern until work measures 3" (7.6cm).

Front

Divide for front: Ch 2, sk the first stitch, sc in the next ch-sp, *ch 1, sk 1 sc, sc in next ch-1 sp; repeat from * 6 more times, turn leaving remaining stitches unworked—16 stitches.

Shape Left Armhole

Row 1 (RS) Ch 1 (does not count as ch-1 sp in pattern), sc2tog over first sc and first ch-1 sp, *ch 1, sk 1 sc, sc in next ch-1 sp; repeat from * across ending sc in ch-2 sp, turn—15 stitches.

Row 2 Work in granite stitch to last ch-1 sp, sc2tog over last ch-1 sp and sc, turn—14 stitches.

Repeat Rows 1–2 of left armhole shaping once, repeat Row 1 once more, turn—11 stitches.

Shape Left V-Neck

Row 1 (WS) Ch 1, sc2tog over first sc and ch-1 sp, *ch 1, sk 1 stitch, sc in next ch-1 sp; repeat from * 3 times, sc in last sc, turn—10 stitches.

Row 2 Ch 2, skip first stitch, sc in next sc, *sc in next ch-1 sp, ch 1, sk 1 stitch; repeat from * 2 times, sc in last sc, turn—9 stitches.

Row 3 Ch 1, sc2tog over first sc and ch-sp, *ch 1, sk 1 stitch, sc in next ch-sp; repeat from * 2 times, sc in last sc, turn—8 stitches.

Row 4 Ch 2, skip first stitch, sc in next sc, *sc in next ch-sp, ch 1, sk 1 stitch; repeat from * once, sc in last sc, turn—7 stitches.

Row 5 Ch 1, sc2tog over first sc and ch-sp, *ch 1, sk 1 stitch, sc in next ch-sp; repeat from * once, sc in last sc, turn—6 stitches.

Row 6 Ch 2, sc in next sc, sc in next ch-sp, ch 1, sk 1 stitch, sc in next ch-sp, sc in last sc. Fasten off.

Shape Right Armhole

With right sides facing, join yarn in beginning chain-2 at the opposite side of the last row of the body worked.

Row 1 (**RS**) Ch 3, sk 1 sc, *sc in next ch-sp, ch 1, sk 1 stitch; rep from * 5 times more, sc in last ch-sp, sc in next sc, turn—16 stitches.

Row 2 Ch 1, sc2tog over first 2 sc, *sc in next ch-sp, ch 1, sk 1 stitch; repeat from * across to ch-3 sp, 2 sc in ch-3 sp, turn—15 stitches.

Row 3 Ch 3, sk first 2 sc, *sc in next ch-sp, ch 1, sk 1 stitch; rep from * across to last ch-sp, sc in next ch-sp, sc2tog over last 2 sc, turn—14 stitches.

Repeat Rows 2–3 of right armhole shaping once, repeat Row 2 once more, turn—11 stitches.

Shape Right V-Neck

Row 1 (RS) Ch 1, sc2tog over first 2 sc, work in granite stitch across ending sc in last sc, turn—10 stitches.

Row 2 Work in granite stitch to last 2 stitches, sc2tog, turn—9 stitches.

Row 3 Ch 1, sc2tog over first 2 sc, work in granite stitch across to last ch-sp, sc in ch-sp, sc in last sc, turn—8 stitches.

Rows 4–5 Repeat Rows 2–3 once—6 stitches.

Row 6 Work one row even in granite stitch across ending sc in the last sc. Fasten off.

Back

With right sides facing, join yarn to first unworked ch-sp of Back, ch 1, sc in same ch-sp, *ch 1, sk 1 sc, sc in the next ch-sp; rep from * 13 times more, sc in the next sc, turn—30 stitches.

Shape Armholes

Row 1 Ch 1, sc2tog over first 2 stitches, work in granite stitch to last 2 stitches, sc2tog, turn—28 stitches.

Repeat Row 1 four more times—20 stitches. Work even in granite stitch for four more rows.

Shape Back Neck

Work in granite stitch over first 6 stitches, turn. Work one more row over those 6 stitches, and fasten off. With right sides facing, join the yarn to the opposite edge of the Back, 6 stitches from end, ch 1, sc in same space, work in granite stitch pattern across to the end, turn. Work over those 6 stitches only for 1 more row, ending with sc in the last stitch. Fasten off.

Assembly

With right sides together, sl st the fronts to back at shoulders.

Patch Pockets (make 2)

Ch 11, sc in second chain from hook and in each chain across, turn—10 sc. Work in granite stitch for 8 more rows. Fasten off. Whipstitch the sides and bottom to the left and right fronts of the vest, using the photo as a guide for placement.

Finishing

Weave in ends. Wet block to measurements. Dry flat. Add fly lure to vest, if desired.

GONE FISHING FLY LURE

Cut a pipe cleaner to a length of about 2" (5cm). Slide bead on and twist the top of the pipe cleaner to secure. Wrap novelty yarn around the pipe cleaner below the bead and use another small piece of pipe cleaner to secure the yarn. Bend the end of the pipe cleaner into a hook shape.

MAKE A CUSTOM-SIZED GONE FISHING VEST

1. Measure your bear's chest at the widest point: _____ *(Chest)*

2. Measure the distance from your bear's hip to underarm: _____ *(Torso Length)*

3. Measure the distance from underarm to shoulder: _____ *(Armhole Depth)*

4. Record stitch gauge (per inch/cm): _____ *(Gauge)*

5. Multiply (Gauge) x (Chest): _____ *(Total Stitches rounded to an even number)*

6. Calculate your foundation chain: (Total Stitches) + 1 = _____ *(Foundation Chain)*

7. Calculate the Front stitches: (Total Stitches) x .25 = _____ *(Front)*

8. Calculate the Back stitches: (Total Stitches) x .50 = _____ *(Back)*

Be sure to round to nearest even number for calculations. Make sure [2x (Front)] + (Back) = _____ *(Total Stitches)*

Work the foundation chain according to your calculation (Foundation Chain), and then work in granite stitch until the vest matches (Torso Length). Work the Fronts and Back according to the pattern and your calculations (Front) and (Back), until the length matches (Armhole Depth). Finish as written in the main pattern.

chapter 4

BACK TO *school*

Although it's hard to leave the fun of summer

behind, the thought of autumn does stir a bit of excitement for

Pearl, Eddie, and Joey. They love heading back to school to be with

classmates, rejoin their sports teams, and crack open new books. Eddie

shows off his school spirit in his Show Your Colors Varsity Jacket (page

52) and keeps it all together with his book bag (page 57). Of course,

the cooler days also mean new fashion opportunities. Pearl loves to

shop for fresh pencils and notebooks, and she earns great marks in her

Schoolgirl Pleated Skirt and Beret (page 60). At the fall formal, she

kicks up her heels in her Let's Dance Ensemble (page 64), complete

with dress, purse, and floral earband.

show your colors VARSITY JACKET AND BOOK BAG

*Go Bears! Eddie proclaims his school spirit in this cozy varsity jacket embla-
zoned with the basketball team's initial. Worked from the bottom up in one
piece to the armholes, the jacket is simply constructed with minimal finishing.*

VARSITY JACKET

Skill Level
Intermediate

Finished Measurements
KEY MEASUREMENT Chest Circumference:
15½" (39.5cm)

Back Neck Width: 4¾" (12 cm)

Length: 6½" (16.5cm)

Sleeve Length: 4½" (11.4 cm)

Sleeve Circumference: 7" (18cm)

Materials
Brown Sheep Lanaloft Sport (100% wool, 145
yards [132.6m], 1.75 oz [50g]):
1 skein 18 Japanese Maple (A), 1 skein 45 Sea
Fog (B), (**2**) fine

U.S. F/5 (3.75mm) crochet hook, or size needed to
obtain gauge

Measuring tape

Yarn needle

Gauge
20 stitches and 13 rows = 4" (10cm) in hdc

Note: *The jacket is worked in one piece from the
bottom up, and then divided at the armholes.
Turning chain does not count as a stitch in half
double crochet rows.*

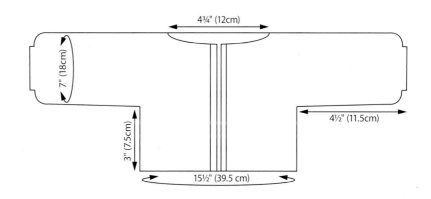

Body

With color A, ch 78.

Row 1 (RS) Hdc in third chain from hook and in each chain across, turn—76 hdc.

Row 2 Ch 2 (counts as hdc here and throughout), hdc across, turn.

Rows 3–10 Repeat Row 2. Fasten off.

Back

With RS facing, join color A 19 stitches in from the right edge.

Row 1 Ch 2, hdc in same hdc and next 37 hdc, turn—38 hdc.

Rows 2–10 Work even in hdc over the back stitches only, turn.

Right Shoulder

Row 11 Ch 2, hdc over first 7 stitches—7 hdc. Do not turn. Fasten off.

Left Shoulder

Row 11 With RS facing, join color A 7 stitches from the end of the same row, ch 2, hdc over last 7 stitches to the end—7 hdc. Fasten off.

Right Front

With RS facing, join color A to the first stitch of Row 10 of Body and work even in hdc over first 18 stitches (leaving 1 stitch unworked between front and back) for 10 rows, turn.

Last row Ch 2, hdc in first 7 stitches only to form Right Front Shoulder. Fasten off.

Left Front

With RS facing, join color A 18 stitches in from the left edge and work even in hdc over 18 stitches only for 10 rows. Fasten off.

Last row Join yarn 7 stitches from the end of the last row, ch 2, and hdc across stitches to form Left Front Shoulder. Fasten off.
Sew shoulder seams with right sides together.

Sleeve

With RS facing, join color B to center stitch at underarm and sl st 36 stitches evenly around the armhole opening, do not join, turn—36 stitches. Ch 2, hdc in each stitch across, turn. Work even in hdc over sleeve stitches for 6 more rows.

Begin Sleeve Shaping

Continue in hdc, decreasing one stitch at the beginning of each row over the next 4 rows—32 stitches. Work even until sleeve measures 4" (10cm) from the beginning. Fasten off. Repeat for second sleeve.

Sleeve Cuffs

The cuffs are worked lengthwise and joined to the sleeve as you go with two slip stitches per join. The first attaches the sides to the top, the second acts as the turning chain. With RS facing, join color A with sl st to the first stitch at the bottom edge of the sleeve, ch 5.

Row 1 Sc in second chain from hook and in each chain across. At the end of the chain, sl st in next two unworked stitches of the sleeve, turn to work back up cuff—4 sc.

Row 2 Sc-blo across, turn.

Row 3 Ch 1, sc-blo across to the sleeve edge, sl st in the next 2 unworked stitches of sleeve, turn.

Repeat Rows 2–3 until the ribbing extends all the way around the sleeve. Slip stitch the edges of the ribbing together. Repeat for second cuff.

Neckband

With RS facing, join color A with sl st to the upper right corner of the neck opening, ch 3.

Row 1 Sc in second chain and third chain from hook, sl st in the next two unworked stitches of the neck, turn to work back up neckband—2 sc.

Row 2 Sc-blo across, turn.

Row 3 Ch 1, sc-blo across to neck edge, sl st in the next 2 unworked stitches of neck, turn. Repeat Rows 2–3 until the ribbing extends all the way around the neck opening.

Ribbed Hem

With RS facing, join color A with sl st to the lower corner of the front left panel, ch 3 and work the bottom edge of the jacket as for the neckband around to the corner of the front right panel. Do not fasten off. Turn to work the right front panel band. With RS facing, sl st evenly up the side edge of the jacket opening to the neck, turn. Work two rows of sc. Sl st final stitch to the side of the neck ribbing. Fasten off.

With RS facing, join color A with sl st to the top corner of left front panel. Work the left front panel band as for the right front panel band.

Varsity Letter

Using color B, Ch 12, turn.

Row 1 Sc in second chain and each chain across, turn—11 sc.

Row 2 Ch 10, sk 5 sc, sc in sixth sc, ch 10, sk next 4 sc, sc in last stitch, turn.

Row 3 Sc in each chain and sc across. Fasten off.

Whipstitch letter B to Jacket using photo as a placement guide.

Finishing

Finishing

Sew sleeve seams with right sides together.

Weave in ends.

|||||||||||||||||||||||||||||||||||||||||||||||||||||||||||||||||||||||||||||||||||||||||||||||||||||||||||||||||||||||||||

MAKE A CUSTOM-SIZED VARSITY JACKET

1. Measure the circumference of your toy's chest at the widest point: _____ *(Chest)*

2. Measure your toy from underarm to hip: _____ *(Underarm)*

3. Measure your toy's arm circumference: _____ *(Arm Circumference)*

4. Divide (Arm Circumference) ÷ 2: _____ *(Armhole Opening)*

5. Record stitch gauge (per inch/cm): _____ *(Gauge)*

6. Multiply your gauge by your chest circumference: (Gauge) x (Chest) = _____ *(Body)*

7. Adjust (Body) to a number divisible by 4: _____ *(Body Adjustment)*

8. Add turning chain: (Body Adjustment) + 2 = _____ *(Foundation Chain)*

9. Calculate Front stitches: (Body Adjustment) ÷ 4 = _____ *(Front)*

10. Calculate Shoulder stitches: [(Front) ÷ 2] – 2 = _____ *(Shoulder)*

Begin your jacket according to the pattern using your calculations for the (Foundation Chain). When beginning to work the Back, skip (Front + 1) stitches at the beginning of the row, and leave (Front + 1) stitches unworked at the end of the row. Be sure to substitute your own calculations for the (Front) and (Shoulders). Follow the pattern, adjusting the length of the body to the (Underarm) and the size of the (Armhole Opening) to your toy's measurements.

Eddie uses this knapsack to tote all his essentials, from pencils to schoolbooks to gym gear. He's the kind of bear who likes to be prepared for anything, and he's just as likely to stash a snack of honey chews in his bag as a baseball or spare rubber band. Made from sturdy wool with a reinforced ribbed base, this bag works up in one piece. The straps double as closure, so there's very little finishing.

Skill Level
Easy

Finished Measurements
Bag Base: 3" (7.5cm) square
Bag Height: 4" (10cm)
Flap Length: 2½" (6.5cm)

Materials
1 skein Knit One Crochet Too Paint Box (100% wool, 100 yds [91.4m], 1.75 oz [50g]), color: #10 walnut rum, (3) light

U.S. G/6 (4mm) crochet hook, or size needed to obtain gauge

Stitch markers

Yarn needle

Gauge
8 stitches and 7½ rounds = 2" (5cm) in esc

Bag Base

Ch 13.

Row 1 Sc in second chain from hook and in each chain across, turn—12 sc.

Row 2 Ch 1, sc-blo across, turn.

Rows 3–11 Repeat Row 2.

Row 12 Ch 1, sc-blo across, do not turn.

Bag Sides

Note: *Worked in spiraled rounds without joins or turns. Place a marker for the beginning of rounds.*

Working one esc in the end of each row, esc evenly along side edge of your base, across the back side of the foundation row, up the second side edge, and back around—48 esc. Continue to work even in esc until bag measures 3½" (9cm) from base.

Eyelet Round

Place a marker at the center of each side, back, and front of your bag. Esc to 3 stitches from center back, *ch 1, sk 1 stitch, esc in the next 4 stitches, ch 1, sk 1 stitch*, esc to 3 stitches from center side, rep from * to *, esc around to 2 stitches before center front, ch 1, sk 1 stitch, esc 2 stitches, ch 1, sk 1 stitch, esc to 3 stitches from the next center side, repeat from * to *—8 chain-spaces. Work 1 final round of esc in each stitch and ch around, ending at left corner edge of bag back, turn.

Flap

Rounds 1–9 Ch 1, esc in 12 stitches across back, turn.

Fasten off.

MAKE A CUSTOM-SIZED BOOK BAG

The bag's finished size is dependent upon the size of the base. Create a chain as wide as you'd like the bag to be. Work in sc-blo to make a base that's approximately square. Follow the instructions for the bag, working the sides to your desired length. Adjust eyelet holes to be spaced evenly on all sides. Make the flap approximately 60 percent of the height of the bag.

Finishing

Strap (make 2)

Ch 51, sc in second chain from hook and in each chain across—50 sc. Fasten off.

Sew one end of each strap to either side of bottom back corners at base. Working one side at a time, feed the straps through the back eyelets, side eyelets, and out through the front eyelets to create the straps and closure. Holding both ends of strap together, secure the ends with an overhand knot.

Edging

Join yarn at the back corner of the bag opening. Ch 1, sc evenly around the opening and the bag flap. Fasten off.

Weave in all ends.

schoolgirl PLEATED SKIRT AND BERET

*Pearl loves autumn—from the beauty of the changing leaves and the crisp,
fresh air to back-to-school notebooks, supplies, and clothes. Her favorite fall
outfit is a classic French-inspired pleated skirt with matching beret, worn
in a jaunty style over one ear. The skirt, worked in soft wool, holds its shape
beautifully and shows off the clever box pleats. The beret is crocheted from
the crown down in a universal pattern that can be easily sized to fit any toy.*

Skill Level

Skirt
Advanced

Beret
Easy

Finished Measurements

Skirt
KEY MEASUREMENT Circumference at waist:
16" (40.6cm)

Circumference at hem: 28" (71cm)

Length: 4½" (11cm)

Beret
KEY MEASUREMENT Diameter at brim: 4" (10cm)

Diameter at crown: 6" (15cm)

Materials

2 skeins Patons Classic Wool (100% wool, 223 yds
(205m), 3.5 oz [100g]), color:
#00230 Bright Red, (4) medium

US H/8 (5mm) crochet hook, or size needed to
obtain gauge

Measuring tape

Yarn needle

Gauge

Skirt
16 stitches and 6 rows = 4" (10cm) in
ldc/sc stitch pattern

Beret
9 stitches and 9½ rows = 2" (5cm) in
sc in the round

Special Stitches

Linked double crochet (ldc) Special
Techniques, page 11.

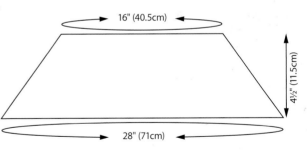

Round 2 Ch 1, sc-blo around, sl st in first sc to join.

Repeat Rounds 1–2 until the skirt measures 4½" (11.5cm) or your desired length.

Fasten off.

Finishing

Sew seam at center back waist. Weave in ends.

SCHOOLGIRL PLEATED SKIRT

Box Pleats

Fsc 50.

Row 1 Ch 1 sc-flo across, turn—50 sc.

Row 2 Ch 1, sc-flo across the remaining loops of the fsc just worked, turn.

Row 3 (Pleat Row) *Row 1 is now facing you.* Ch 1, *[sc in the next stitch of both Rows 1 and 2, *at the same time*, joining the two rows together] twice, sc-flo in next 3 stitches of Row 1 only, turn work, sc the middle loops of

Rows 1 and 2 together in last 3 stitches, turn, sc remaining loops of same 3 stitches of Row 2 to complete the pleat; repeat from * across the row—110 stitches.

Join to work in the round. The remainder of the skirt is worked in joined rounds without turning. Turning chains are *not* counted as stitches.

Round 1 Ch 3, ldc in each stitch around, sl st in first ldc to join.

SCHOOLGIRL BERET

Begin as for Basic Hat Technique (page 11), working increases until the crown is 6" (15cm) in diameter or 150 percent of the head size you're trying to fit.

Beret Sides

Rounds 1–3 Sc in each stitch around.

Round 4 *Sc2tog; rep from * around.

Rounds 5–8 Sc in each stitch around.

Fasten off. Weave in ends.

MAKE A CUSTOM-SIZED SCHOOLGIRL PLEATED SKIRT

1. Measure your toy's waist circumference:

_____ *(Waist)*

2. Record stitch gauge (per inch/cm):

_____ *(Gauge)*

3. Multiply your gauge by your waist circumference: (Gauge) x (Waist) =

_____ *(Preliminary Stitch Count)*

4. Take this result and round to the nearest multiple of 5:

_____ *(Foundation Single Crochet)*

Work the pattern as written, substituting your foundation calculations. Work the skirt to a length appropriate for your toy. Feel free to be creative and change the stitch pattern for the skirt as well.

Recommended Reading: box pleats

I learned to create box pleats from Belinda "Bendy" Carter's book Crochet on the Edge *(Annie's Attic, 2006), and it's a great resource for any crocheter. The techniques collected in this book are specifically for use in decorative edgings but their possibilities extend far beyond the edges of garments—as shown in this skirt.*

let's dance ENSEMBLE

by guest designer Robyn Chachula

Always ready for a party, Pearl loves to dress her best. She loves the way the skirt on this floral motif frock swings on the dance floor. Together with the wristlet purse and floral earband, she's dressed to the nines and ready to dance the night away. Created by guest designer Robyn Chachula, this pretty dress is crocheted using circular motifs that are joined as you work.

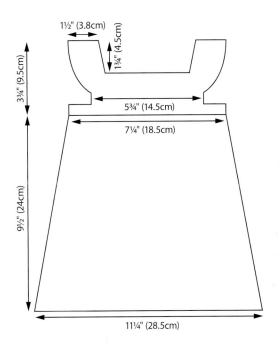

Skill level
Advanced

Finished Measurements

Dress
Chest Circumference: 14½" (37cm)
Length: 13" (33cm)
Armhole: 3¼" (8cm)

Note: *Because of the construction method, there is no Key Measurement for the Dress.*

Earband
Circumference: 6½" (16.5cm)

Wristlet Purse
Length: 2" (5cm)
Width: 3" (7.5cm)
Strap: 3" (7.5cm)

Materials
U.S. F/5 (3.75mm) and U.S. 7 (4.5mm)
or sizes needed to obtain gauge

Yarn needle

Dress
2 hanks Southwest Trading Co. Vickie Howell Signature Collection Love, (70% Bamboo, 30% Silk, 90m [98 yds]/1.75oz [50g]), color:
Ennis & Jack, (3) light

Blocking pins

(4) ¼" (6mm) pearl buttons

Matching sewing thread and needle

Earband and Wristlet Purse
30 yds Southwest Trading Co. Vickie Howell Signature Collection Love, (70% Bamboo, 30% Silk, 90m [98 yds]/1.75oz [50g]), color:
Ennis & Jack, (3) light

Gauge
Granny Motif = 2¼" (5.5cm) in diameter with smaller hook, 2½" (6.5cm) in diameter with larger hook
7½ stitches and 8 rows = 2" (5cm) in hdc with larger hook

LET'S DANCE DRESS

Note: *Make one motif and then connect the remaining motifs as you crochet, following the joining directions.*

Skirt

Granny Motif (Make 1 with smaller hook)

Ch 5, sl st to first chain to form ring.

Round 1 (RS) Ch 1, *sc in ring, ch 3, rep from * 6 more times, sc in ring, ch 1, hdc to first sc, do not turn—8 sc.

Round 2 Ch 1, sc in top of hdc, *ch 4, sc in next ch-3 sp; rep from * around, ch 2, hdc to first sc, do not turn—8 chain-spaces.

Round 3 Ch 1, sc in top of hdc, *ch 5, sc in next ch-4 sp; rep from * around, ch 5, sl st to first sc, fasten off.

Make and Join: (Make and join 17 with smaller hook and 18 with larger hook following the Granny Motif Layout)

Joining Motifs a–j Using the smaller hook, follow directions for Granny Motif to Round 2. Refer to Joining Two Motifs for assistance.

Round 3 Follow Round 3 directions to first adjoining ch-5 sp, ch 2, sl st to adjoining motif's chain-5 space, ch 2, sc in next chain-4 space, ch 2, sl st to adjoining motif's next chain-5 space, ch 2, continue in Round 3 directions to end, fasten off.

Joining Motifs 1–27 Follow directions for Joining Motifs a–j for joining motifs, by connecting all chain-5 spaces on all adjoining motifs. Use the larger hook for motifs 10–27. Refer to Joining More Motifs for assistance.

Blocking and Seaming Skirt

Pin motifs to schematic size. Spray with water and allow to dry. To connect the back seam, unravel the last row of one motif and join in the same manner as joining above.

Bodice

With RS facing, join yarn with the larger hook to the center back in chain-5 space at the left of the center sc with sl st.

Row 1 Ch 2 (counts as hdc here and throughout), 2 hdc in same chain-5 space, 3 hdc in next chain-5 space and each chain-5 space across, turn—54 hdc.

Row 2 Ch 2 (counts as hdc), *hdc between next 2 hdc; repeat from * across to end, turn.

Back Left Panel

Row 1 Ch 2, *hdc between next 2 hdc, repeat from * 9 more times, leave remaining stitches unworked, turn—11 hdc.

Row 2 Ch 2, *hdc between next 2 hdc, repeat from * across to end, turn.

Repeat Row 2 four more times, fasten off.

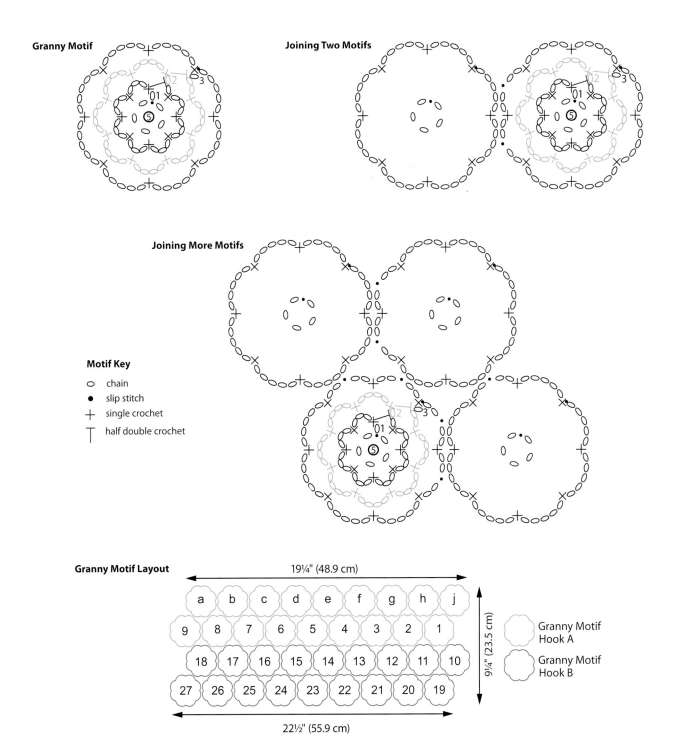

Granny Motif

Joining Two Motifs

Joining More Motifs

Motif Key

○ chain
● slip stitch
+ single crochet
⊤ half double crochet

Granny Motif Layout

19¼" (48.9 cm)

| a | b | c | d | e | f | g | h | j |

| 9 | 8 | 7 | 6 | 5 | 4 | 3 | 2 | 1 |

| 18 | 17 | 16 | 15 | 14 | 13 | 12 | 11 | 10 |

| 27 | 26 | 25 | 24 | 23 | 22 | 21 | 20 | 19 |

9¼" (23.5 cm)

22½" (55.9 cm)

Granny Motif Hook A

Granny Motif Hook B

Front Panel

Row 1 With RS facing, skip 5 hdc from end of Row 1 of back left panel, join yarn with sl st, ch 2, *hdc between next 2 hdc; repeat from * 20 more times, leave remaining stitches unworked, turn—22 hdc.

Row 2 Ch 2, *hdc between next 2 hdc; repeat from * across to end, turn.

Repeat Row 2 four more times, fasten off.

Back Right Panel

Row 1 With RS facing, skip 5 hdc from end of Row 1 of front panel, join yarn with sl st, ch 2, *hdc between next 2 hdc; rep from * 9 more times, leave remaining stitches unworked, turn—11 hdc.

Row 2 Ch 2, *hdc between next 2 hdc; repeat from * across to end, turn.

Repeat Row 2 four more times, fasten off.

Sleeves

With wrong sides facing, join yarn with the larger hook to the upper right corner of back panel with sl st.

Row 1 Ch 14, sl st to upper right corner of front panel, sl st to first row end of arm opening of front panel, turn.

Row 2 Skip sl sts, hdc in each ch across to end, sl st to first 2 row ends of arm opening of back panel (once to join row and once for turning chain), turn—14 hdc.

Row 3 Skip sl sts, *hdc between next 2 hdc; repeat from * across to end, sl st to next 2 row ends of arm opening of front panel, turn.

Row 4 Ch 3, sl to first hdc, *ch 3, sl st to next hdc; repeat from * across to end, ch 3, sl st to next 2 row ends of arm opening of back panel, turn.

Row 5 Ch 3, sl to first chain-3 space, *ch 5, sl st to next chain-3 space; repeat from * across to end, ch 3, sl st to next row end of arm opening of front panel, fasten off.

Turn work 180 degrees so foundation chain is facing up.

Row 6 With larger hook, join yarn one hdc from ch, *hdc between next 2 hdc; repeat from * across to end, sl st to neck of back panel twice, turn.

Row 7 Skip slip stitches, *hdc between next 2 hdc; repeat from * across to end, sl st to neck of front panel, fasten off.

Repeat for second sleeve, except begin by joining yarn to wrong side of front panel first.

||||||||||||||||||||||||||||||||||||||||||||||||||||||||||||||||||||||||||||||||||||

MAKE A CUSTOM-SIZED LET'S DANCE DRESS

1. Measure the circumference of your toy's chest:

_____ *(Chest)*

2. Divide (Chest) by 2.25 (one small motif) to get number of motifs for upper row of skirt, then round to next whole number:

_____ *(Small Motifs)*

This is the same number of motifs worked with larger hook:

_____ *(Large Motifs)*

3. Work the skirt and the first two rounds of Bodice as for pattern and layout, using your number for (Small Motifs).

4. Note number of stitches worked in last row of bodice:

_____ *(Bodice)*

5. Multiply (Bodice) stitches x .1, rounded to the next whole number:

_____ *(Right and Left Armhole Stitches)*

6. Subtract (Right and Left Armhole Stitches) – (Bodice):

_____ *(Front Panel)*

7. Divide (Front Panel) ÷ 2:

_____ *(Back Right and Back Left panel)*

8. Measure the armhole depth:

_____ *(Armhole)*

Continue bodice as for pattern skipping (Right and Left Armhole Stitches) at the beginning of (Front Panel) and (Back Right Panel) and working the (Back/Left) and (Front Panel) using your calculations. Work armhole according to your (Armhole) calculation.

Neck Edging

With RS facing, join yarn with the larger hook to the bottom of the back left panel with sl st. Ch 1, sc evenly up the edge of the back left panel to neck, turn work 90 degrees, and sl st evenly around the neck to the opposite back right panel, turn work 90 degrees, sc evenly down the back right panel and around the top of skirt to first sc, sl st to first sc, do not turn.

Make Buttonholes

Ch 2, *sl st in next 2 stitches, ch 2, repeat from * twice more, sl st in the last stitches to neck, fasten off.

Finishing

Sew pearl buttons to opposite panel with matching thread and sewing needle at buttonhole locations.

LET'S DANCE EARBAND

Note: *To customize the size of the earband, simply adjust the chain following Round 2 to fit around your bear's ear. (Or you can make it even larger to create a headband instead of an earband).*

Flower Motif

○ chain
● slip stitch
+ single crochet
⊤ half double crochet

Flower Motif (make 1)

Ch 5 with larger hook, sl st to the first chain to form ring.

Round 1 (RS) Ch 1, *sc in ring, ch 3, rep from * 7 more times, sl st to first sc, do not turn—8 sc.

Round 2 [Sl st, sc, 3 hdc, sc, sl st] in each chain-3 space around, sl st to first sc, do not turn.

Ch 30, sl st to opposite side of flower, fasten off. Join yarn to opposite side of same petal with sl st, ch 30, sl st to opposite side of flower, fasten off.

LET'S DANCE WRISTLET PURSE

Note: *To customize the purse, just adjust the length of the strap to fit around the wrist of your bear (repeating Row 2 for as many rows as necessary).*

Ch 20 with larger hook.

Row 1 (RS) Hdc in third chain from hook (skipped ch, count as hdc), hdc in next chain and each chain across, turn—19 hdc.

Row 2 Ch 2 (counts as hdc), *hdc between next 2 hdc; repeat from * across to end, turn. Repeat Row 2 nine more times, fasten off. Fold body in half lengthwise, join yarn to left side, ch 1, *working through both sides at the same time*, sc across left side, fasten off.

Flap

Join yarn to right side at folded edge, ch 1.

Row 1 (RS) Working through both sides at the same time, sc up right side, 2 sc at top purse opening, working through back panel only, sc across back evenly, turn—11 stitches.

Row 2 Ch 2 (counts as hdc), working across back panel only, hdc in next sc and each sc across, turn.

Row 3 Ch 2 (counts as hdc), *hdc between next 2 hdc; repeat from * across to end, turn.

Row 4 Ch 1, sc in first hdc, *ch 3, sk next hdc, sc in next hdc; repeat from * across to last 2 hdc, ch 1, hdc in last hdc, turn.

Row 5 Ch 1, sc in hdc, *ch 3, sc in next ch-3 sp; repeat from * across to last ch-3 sp, ch 1,

hdc in last ch-3 sp, turn.

Row 6 Ch 1, sc in hdc, *ch 3, sc in next ch-3 sp; repeat from * across to last ch-3 sp, ch 3, sc in last ch-3 sp, fasten off.

With larger hook, make one flower motif (page 70) and sew to front of flap.

Strap

Join yarn to one side at seam 4 stitches from bottom with sl st.

Row 1 (RS) Ch 1, sc in next 3 stitches of seam, turn—3 sc.

Row 2 Ch 1, sc in each sc across, turn.

Repeat Row 2 until strap is as long as the width of the purse.

Join strap to purse by slip stitching to corresponding stitches at opposite seam edge.

chapter 5

STAYING WARM IN *winter*

For our favorite teddies, cold winter weather

brings thoughts of hibernation, but Pearl, Eddie, and Joey still enjoy

a little fun in the snow, too. Pearl wards off the winter chill with her

Cozy Turtleneck (page 74) before snuggling down to sleep in her warm

Long Winter's Nap Nightgown and Cap (page 82). Her brother, Eddie,

loves winter and can be found building snow forts and sledding in his

traditionally inspired Fair Isle Sweater (page 78). If Joey has to leave

the comfort of his den during winter it must be to find a snack—and

he's happy to strap on his ice skates for a visit to his favorite fishing

hole. To stay warm he'll don his Fisherman's Sweater (page 88) before

heading out in the elements.

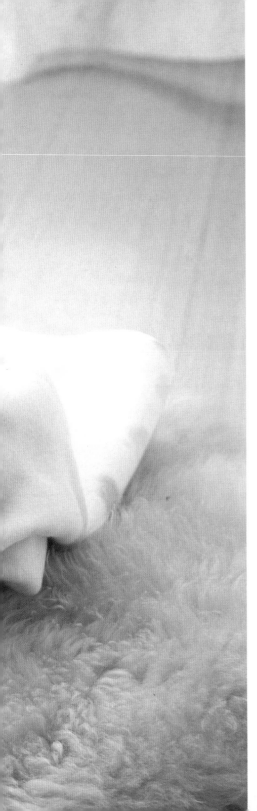

cozy TURTLENECK

On the iciest of winter days, Pearl prefers to stay indoors with a cup of cocoa, her favorite book, and this warm turtleneck sweater. The sideways ribbed texture gives extra warmth and stretch to the fabric. The sweater is worked modularly in one piece; the only finishing is crocheting the under-arm and side seams.

Skill Level
Easy

Finished Measurements
KEY MEASUREMENT Length including turtleneck:
7" (18cm)

Chest Circumference: 16" (40.5cm)

Neck Circumference: 14" (35.5cm)

Shoulder to Waist Length: 5" (12.5cm)

Sleeve Length: 3" (7.5cm)

Armhole Depth: 3" (7.5cm)

Length from Underarm to Hem: 2" (5cm)

Materials
1 skein Malabrigo Merino Worsted (100% merino wool, 215 yards [196m], 3.5 oz [100g]), color: #41 Burgundy, (3) light

US H/8 (5mm) crochet hook, or size needed to obtain gauge

Yarn needle

Gauge
17 stitches and 12 rows = 4" (10cm) in hdc-blo

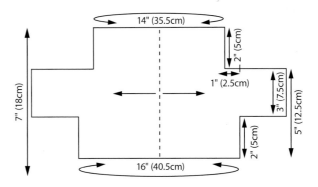

Note: *The sweater begins at the center front or back—the neck is worked out on either side in modular crochet style (page 25) from the center for the front and back and then joined to work the shoulders/sides and sleeves.*

Center Panel (make 2)

Fsc 30. Ch 2 (does not count as a stitch), hdc-blo in each stitch across, turn—30 hdc. Work in hdc-blo until piece measures half the width of the back of the toy's neck. Fasten off.

Join yarn to the first stitch on the opposite side of the foundation row. Work an equal number of rows to the first half in hdc-blo. Fasten off.

Close Turtleneck

With front and back center panels held together and with right sides facing each other, sc the two pieces together on either side for 2" (5cm) from one edge to create the turtleneck. Fasten off. Repeat for the second side.

Create Shoulders/Sides

Join yarn to first stitch of center panel, on either side of turtleneck, work 3 rows, or until you've added 1" (2.5cm) in hdc-blo. Fasten off. Repeat for second side of turtleneck.

Sleeves

Join yarn 2" (5cm) from bottom edge, work in hdc-blo over next 6" (15cm), turn leaving remaining 2" (5cm) unworked. Work in hdc-blo on sleeve stitches only for 3" (7.5cm). Fasten off. Repeat for second side.

Finishing

Fold sweater in half with right sides together, sc side and sleeve seams closed in one line. Weave in ends.

MAKE A CUSTOM-SIZED COZY TURTLENECK

1. Measure your toy's neck width: _____ *(Neck Width)*

2. Measure the length from your toy's shoulder to hip: _____ *(Torso Length)*

3. Add approx. 2" (5cm) to the (Torso Length) for the turtleneck: _____ *(Total Length)*

4. Record stitch gauge (per inch/cm): _____ *(Gauge)*

5. Multiply your gauge by your key measurement: (Gauge) x (Total Length) = _____ *(Foundation Single Crochet)*

6. Measure your toy's length from shoulder to underarm: _____ *(Armhole Depth)*

7. Multiply (Armhole Depth) x 2: _____ *(Sleeve Width)*

8. Measure the distance from underarm to hem:

_____ *(Skipped Side Stitches before Sleeve Width)*

9. Measure your toy's shoulder if it has one (If it does not, just work 2 rows for the shoulder.):

_____ *(Shoulder Rows)*

10. Measure your toy's arm length (from shoulder):

_____ *(Sleeve Length)*

Work the foundation stitches (Foundation Single Crochet) according to your calculations, then follow the pattern, working the first half of the side panel until it measures half your toy's (Neck Width). Continue following the pattern using your measurements. Work the shoulder according to your measurements or work 2 rows, if, like Pearl, your toy has no measurable shoulder. Skip stitches according to your measurements to center the sleeves and work the sleeves to the length you desire. Finish according to the pattern.

fair isle SWEATER

Crocheted by Eddie's Norwegian Bestemor Bjørn (Grandma Bear), this sweater is inspired by traditional Scandinavian design. With a round yoke worked from the neck down, the sweater features shifting two-color patterns worked in stranded Fair Isle or jacquard crochet. While the technique may appear daunting, it's really quite easy. If you've made a few hats, you'll have gotten the hang of increasing in the round and this sweater's construction will be a snap.

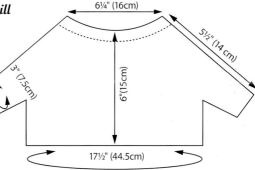

Skill Level
Advanced

Finished Measurements
KEY MEASUREMENT Chest circumference: 17½" (44.5cm)

Back Neck Width: 6¼" (16cm)

Length (including neck and waistband): 6" (15cm)

Sleeve Length (from neck): 5½" (14cm)

Yoke Depth: 4¼" (11cm)

Materials
Mission Falls 1824 Wool (100% merino superwash, 87 yards [78m], 1.76 oz [50g]):
1 skein 004 Charcoal (A), 1 skein 011 Poppy (B), 1 skein 028 Pistachio (C), 1 skein 013 Curry (D), (4) medium

U.S. I/9 (5.5mm) crochet hook, or size needed to obtain gauge

Yarn needle

Gauge
15½ stitches and 14 rows = 4" (10cm) in sc-blo

Ribbed Neckband

With color A, ch 5.

Row 1 Sc in second chain from hook and each chain across, turn—4 sc.

Row 2 Ch 1, sc-blo across, turn.

Repeat Row 2 for a total of 44 rows from beginning, until the neckband measures 12½" unstretched.

Yoke

Round 1 Ch 1, sc around side edge of neckband working one stitch for every row of the neckband, sl st in the first sc to join, do not turn—44 sc. Place a marker to denote the center back.

Round 2 Ch 1, *sc-blo in next 3 stitches, 2 sc-blo in next st, repeat from * around, sl st in the first sc to join—55 sc.

Begin Yoke Chart

Continuing to work the yoke of the sweater in sc-blo, follow the chart for placement of colors and yoke increases. *At the same time* continue to shape yoke as follows:

Round 1 Ch 1, sc-blo evenly around, sl st in first sc to join.

Round 2 Ch 1, sc in first 4 stitches, 2 sc in next stitch, *sc in next 4 stitches, 2 sc in next stitch; repeat from * around, sl st in first sc to join—66 sc.

Round 3 Repeat Round 1.

Round 4 Ch 1, *2 sc in next st, sc in next 5 stitches; repeat from * around, ending sc in last 4 sts, sl st in first sc to join—77 sc.

Rounds 5–7 Repeat Round 1.

Round 8 Ch 1, sc in first 5 stitches, *2 sc in next stitch, sc in next 6 stitches; repeat from * around, ending sc in last stitch, sl st in first sc to join—88 sc.

Round 9 Work one more round, adding two stitches evenly around to bring the stitch count to 90.

Form Armholes

Beginning at center back marker with color C, sc-blo across the first 15 stitches, ch 3, sk 14 stitches, sc-blo across next 31 stitches, ch 3, sk 14 stitches, sc-blo to the end of the round, sl st in first sc to join—62 sc and 6 ch.

Next round Ch 1, sc-blo in each stitch and ch around, sl st in first sc to join—66 sc. Work 2 more rounds even in sc-blo. Fasten off.

Sleeves

Join color C at underarm, ch 1, work in spiraled rounds of sc-blo until sleeve measures 5½" (14cm) from neck edge. Fasten off. Repeat for second sleeve.

Cuffs

The cuffs are worked lengthwise, and joined to the sleeve as you go with 2 slip stitches per join. The first attaches the sides to the top, the second acts as the turning chain.

With color A, join yarn to the edge of the sleeve at the underarm with a sl st, ch 3.

Row 1 Sc in second chain from hook and in the third—2 sc. Sl st in the next two unworked stitches of the sleeve. Turn to work back up the cuff.

Row 2 Sc-blo in each stitch of cuff, turn.

Row 3 Ch 1, sc-blo across to the sleeve edge, sl st in the next 2 unworked stitches of the sleeve, turn.

Repeat Rows 2–3 until the ribbing extends all the way around the sleeve. Sl st the edges of the ribbing together. Repeat for the second cuff.

Waistband

Join color A at center back. Work as for cuffs, beginning with a ch 4.

Finishing

Weave in ends.

MAKE A CUSTOM-SIZED FAIR ISLE SWEATER

Begin ribbing as for the pattern, working the ribbed neckband until it comfortably fits around your toy's neck unstretched. Work Round 1 as for Yoke, working one stitch into each row edge. On the second round, work sc-blo, increasing your total stitches to a multiple of 5:

_____ (Total Stitches)

Begin the Yoke Chart, increasing the yoke evenly until the yoke fits comfortably over your toy's arms.

Note: If the chart cannot be completed before the sweater fits your toy, consider abbreviating the chart or working the sweater in a lighter-weight yarn.

Begin to form the armholes:

1. Adjust stitch count of the body to a multiple of 6:

_____ (Yoke Stitches)

2. Multiply the (Yoke Stitches) by 35 percent each for front and back stitches: (Yoke Stitches) x .35 =

_____(Front and Back Stitches [each])

3. Multiply the Yoke stitches by 15 percent (rounded to the nearest whole number) to calculate how many stitches to skip for each armhole: (Yoke Stitches) x .15 =

_____ (Armhole Stitches)

Note: A ch 3 as specified in the main pattern is sufficient for any toy or doll's armhole.

Work even on the remaining stitches until the sweater is the right length for your toy. Work armholes as for the pattern using your calculations for (Front), (Back), and (Armhole Stitches). Work the sleeves and bands according to the pattern, adjusting the sleeve length to fit your toy.

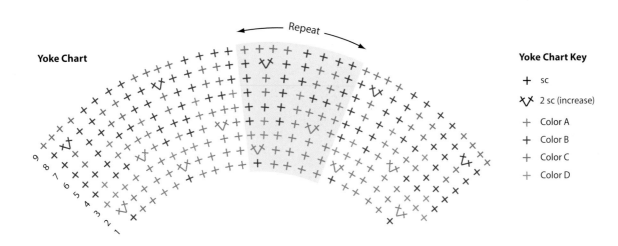

Yoke Chart

Repeat

Yoke Chart Key

+   sc

XX   2 sc (increase)

+   Color A

+   Color B

+   Color C

+   Color D

long winter's nap NIGHTGOWN AND CAP

When Pearl gets ready for hibernation, she likes to be warm. Fortunately, her alpaca nightgown and cap can keep out any chill—and still give her ears some wiggle room. This lovely blue gown is worked in top-down raglan style with textured stitches that offer interest and drape. Whimsical freehand chain embroidery adorns the nightcap and coordinates with the gown's simple but striking two-color single crochet edged hem.

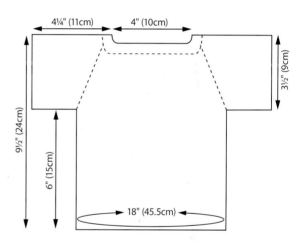

Skill Level

Nightgown
Intermediate

Cap
Easy

Finished Measurements

Nightgown
KEY MEASUREMENT Neckband Circumference: 13¼" (33.5cm)

Length: 9½" (24cm)

Sleeve Length (from neck): 4¼" (11cm)

Distance from Neckband to Underarm (Raglan Seam Length): 3½" (9cm)

Cap
KEY MEASUREMENT Circumference: 13" (33cm)

Length: 9" (23cm)

Materials
Blue Sky Alpacas Mélange (100% alpaca, 110 yards [100m], 1.76 oz [50g]), color: 2 skeins #800 cornflower (A), 1 skein #806 salsa (B), (**2**) fine (Only a few yards of color B is needed for these projects.)

U.S. E/4 (3.5mm) crochet hook, or size needed to obtain gauge

Stitch markers in varying colors

Measuring tape

Yarn needle

½" (13mm) shank button

Matching sewing thread and needle

Gauge
20 stitches and 16 rows = 4" (10cm) in sc-blo in the round

Neckband Row Gauge: 20 rows = 4" (10cm) in sc-blo

Begin Raglan Increases

Ch 1, *sc-blo to first marker, work 3 sc in marked stitch, and move marker to middle stitch of 3 sc just worked; repeat from * around, sc to the end of the round—74 sc. Repeat the last round 10 more times or until the sleeve portion of the shirt just fits around the bear's arm—154 sc.

Form Armholes

Sc-blo to first marker, work 2 sc in the marked stitch, sl st to the next marked stitch, work 2 sc in same stitch, sc to next marker, work 2 sc in marked stitch, sl st to next marked stitch, work 2 sc in same stitch, sc to the end of the round, change to color B in the last stitch—92 sc. Remove raglan increase markers.

Skirt

Note: *In dc-blo rounds, the turning chain does not count as a stitch and is not worked in the following round. The skirt is worked in joined rounds without turning.*

Round 1 With color B, ch 3 (does not count as stitch), dc in first sc, dc-blo in each sc around, skipping sl st's for armholes, sl st in first dc to join—92 dc.

Round 2 Work as for Round 1, changing to color A in the last stitch of the round.

Round 3 With color A, ch 3, dc in first stitch, dc-blo around, sl st in 1st dc to join.

Work as for Round 3 until skirt measures 6" (15cm) from the armholes.

LONG WINTER'S NAP NIGHTGOWN

Ribbed Neckband

With color A, ch 3.

Row 1 Sc in second chain from hook and next chain, turn—2 sc.

Row 2 Ch 1, sc-blo across, turn.

Repeat Row 2 for a total of 66 rows.

Make Buttonhole

At center back of the neckband, join color A to one side of the ribbing with a sl st. Ch 3. Sl st to opposite end of the same ribbing row. Fasten off.

Yoke

Note: *The raglan portion of the nightgown is worked in spiraled rounds without turns or joins.*

Round 1 Ch 1, sc across long edge of neckband working 1 sc for every row end—66 sc. Place a marker to denote the center back.

Round 2 Ch 1, sc-blo around.

Setup for Raglan Increases

Beginning at center back, count 11 stitches, place marker in the last stitch, count 11 more stitches, place marker in the last stitch, count 22 stitches, place marker in the last stitch, count 11 stitches, place marker in the last stitch. Remove the center back marker.

Skirt Edging

With color A ch 1, sc in the first stitch, change to color B, *sc with color B, sc with color A; repeat from * around, ending in color B, sl st in first sc to join. Fasten off.

Sleeves

Join color A at underarm, ch 2, sc in each sl st around—33 sc. Work in spiraled rounds of sc-blo until sleeve measures 4¼" (11cm) from neck edge. Repeat for the second sleeve.

Finishing

Weave in ends.

LONG WINTER'S NAP CAP

Note: *The cap is worked from the brim to the point in the round, without turns or joins after the first round.*

With color A, ch 65.

Round 1 Sc in the second chain from the hook and in each chain across, turn, sl st in first sc to join, being careful not to twist your work, do not turn, place a marker in the first stitch to help keep track of rounds—64 sc.
Round 2 Ch 1, sc-flo in each stitch around.
Rounds 3–4 Work even in sc-flo for 2 more rounds.

Ear Holes

Place two markers (of a different color than round-tracking marker) opposite each other

in the round. Sc-flo to 5 stitches before the marker, ch 16, skip 10 stitches, sc-flo in sixth stitch after marker to make the first Ear Hole. Sc-flo to 5 stitches before second marker and work as for first Ear Hole—44 sc and 32 chain. Continue to sc-flo around, working sc in each chain made on the previous round—76 stitches. Remove ear markers, leaving round-tracking marker.

Cap Decreases

Place one marker every 19 stitches to divide

MAKE A CUSTOM-SIZED NIGHTGOWN

Begin as written in the pattern. Work the neckband until it fits around your toy's neck unstretched. Count the rows.

1. Adjust the row count to a multiple of 6 (adding rows is preferable to removing them unless you only need to remove 1 or 2). Make a note of your (Final Row Count):

_____

Continue as for pattern working one sc in each row end of the neckband.

2. When getting ready to setup for the raglan increases, divide the (Final Row Count) by six: (Final Row Count) ÷ 6 =

_____ *(N)*

Beginning at center back, count (N) stitches, place marker in the last stitch, count (N) more stitches, place marker in the last stitch, count (N x 2) stitches, place marker in the last stitch, count (N) stitches, place a marker in the last stitch. Remove the center back marker. Follow the remainder of the pattern as written, adjusting the skirt and sleeve lengths to fit your toy.

the hat into 4 sections. Decrease every other round, working sc-flo2tog at marked stitch until 4 stitches remain. Move markers up after each decrease. Fasten off. Weave tail through remaining stitches and draw to close opening.

Finishing

Sew button with matching thread and sewing needle at buttonhole location. Weave in ends.

MAKE A CUSTOM-SIZED NIGHT CAP

1. Measure your toy's head under the ears:

_____ *(Head Circumference)*

2. Measure the distance around your toy's ear:

_____ *(Ear Circumference)*

3. Record stitch gauge (per inch/cm):

_____ *(Gauge)*

4. Multiply your gauge by your key measurement: (Gauge) x (Head Circumference) =

_____ *(Total Stitches)*

5. Take this result, round to the nearest multiple of 4 and add 1 for your foundation chain:
[(Total Stitches) rounded to nearest multiple of 4] + 1 =

_____ *(Foundation Chain)*

6. Calculate Ear Stitches: (Ear Circumference) x Gauge =

_____ *(Ear Hole Chain Stitches)*

7. Calculate Skipped Stitches: (Ear Circumference) x .66 =

_____ *(Skipped Stitches rounded to nearest whole number)*

8. Calculate Decrease Placement: Total Stitches x .25 =

_____ *(Decrease Placement rounded to nearest whole number)*

Work the foundation chain according to your calculations, and then follow the pattern, substituting your own calculations for (Ear Hole Chain Stitches), (Skipped Stitches), and (Decrease Placement).

Tassel

Use a credit card as a template. Wrap yarns A and B the long way around the card until you have about 30 wraps. Thread a piece of yarn through the wraps at the top of the card and tie it off. Remove the tied loops from the card. Tie another piece of yarn tightly around the loops about ½" (13mm) down from the tied off section. Wrap yarn several times around to create a decorative top to the tassel. Leave an 8" (20.5cm) tail. Use the tail to tie the tassel to the tip of the hat. Follow the photo as a guide. Trim the tassel to your desired length.

Freehand Chain Embroidery

Thread a yarn needle with a 36"- (91cm)-long piece of color B with a knot at the end. Bring the needle up from the wrong side of the work to the right side, and bring it back down, just to the left of where it came up, creating a small chain loop (use your finger to hold the loop in place if necessary). Bring the needle back up to the right side at the top of the loop, securing it, and then bring it back down just to the left of where it came up to make the next chain loop. Continue as such around the hat. You can embellish the hat with any design you'd like, beginning at the bottom of the hat and continuing up in a free-form design. Or you can use the photo as a guide.

Fisherman's SWEATER

by guest designer Drew Emborsky

When Joey pokes his head out of the den during the winter, he likes to be warm and fashionable. Fortunately, this Aran-inspired fisherman's sweater both holds the icy temperatures at bay and keeps Joey looking great. Guest designer Drew Emborsky specializes in creating cozy designs any bear—or human—in your life will love.

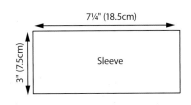

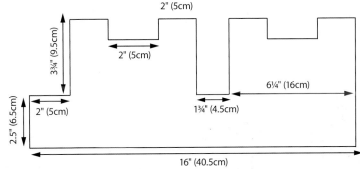

Skill Level
Advanced

Finished Measurements
Chest/waist: 16" (40.5cm)

Neck: 6½" (15cm)

Arm length: 3" (7.5cm)

Arm circumference: 7¼" (18.5cm)

Note: *There is no key measurement for this sweater.*

Materials
2 hanks Vermont Organic Fiber Company O-Wool Classic 2-Ply (100% organic merino wool, 198yds [181m], 1.75oz [50g]), color: #1000 Natural, **1** superfine

U.S. F/5 (3.75mm) crochet hook, or size needed to obtain gauge

Yarn needle

½" (13mm) button in coordinating color

Gauge
24 stitches x 13 rows = 4" (10cm) in gauge swatch

Gauge swatch

Ch 28.

Row 1 Dc in fourth chain from hook and in each chain across, turn—26 dc.

Row 2 Ch 2 (counts as hdc), *fpdc around next 2 dc, bpdc around next 2 dc; rep from * across, ending with hdc in tch, turn.

Rows 3–17 Repeat Row 2.

Note: *The front, back, and sides of the sweater are worked flat as one piece and then seamed together on the side.*

Because of the complexity of the Aran patterning, this sweater is only offered in the standard 16"–18" (40.5cm–45.5cm) toy size. To vary the size of the sweater, try changing hook sizes and yarn weight.

Body

Ch 98.

Row 1 (RS) Dc into fourth chain from hook and in each chain across, turn—96 dc.

Row 2 Ch 2 (counts as hdc now and throughout), *bpdc around next dc, fpdc around next dc; repeat from * across ending with hdc in last stitch, turn.

Row 3 Ch 2, *cba, [bpdc 2, cba] twice, fpdc 3, [bpdc 3, fpdc 3] twice, [cba, bpdc 2] three times, fpdc 2, bpdc 4, fpdc 2, bpdc 2, repeat from * once more, ending with hdc in last stitch, turn.

Row 4 Ch 2, fpdc around the post of every front raised stitch, bpdc around the post of every back raised stitch, hdc in last stitch, turn.

Row 5 Ch 2, *cba, [bpdc 2, cba] twice, bpdc 3, [fpdc 3, bpdc 3] twice, [cba, bpdc 2] twice, cba, bpdc, cbb, cbc, bpdc 2, cbb, cbc, bpdc, repeat from * once more, ending with hdc in last stitch, turn.

Row 6 Repeat Row 4.

Row 7 Ch 2, *cba, [bpdc 2, cba] twice, fpdc 3, [bpdc 3, fpdc 3] twice, [cba, bpdc 2] twice, cba, bpdc, fpdc, bpdc 2, cbc, cbb, bpdc 2, fpdc, bpdc, repeat from * once more ending with hdc in last stitch, turn.

Row 8 Repeat Row 4.

Shape Front Armhole

Row 1 (RS) Ch 2, cba, [bpdc 2, cba] twice, bpdc 3, [fpdc 3, bpdc 3] twice, [cba, bpdc 2] twice, cba, hdc in next stitch, leave remaining stitches unworked, turn—37 stitches.

Row 2 Repeat Row 4 of Body.

Row 3 Ch 2, cba, [bpdc 2, cba] twice, fpdc 3, [bpdc 3, fpdc 3] twice, [cba, bpdc 2] twice, cba, hdc in last stitch, turn.

Row 4 Repeat Row 4 of Body.

Row 5 Ch 2, cba, [bpdc 2, cba] twice, bpdc 3, [fpdc 3, bpdc 3] twice, [cba, bpdc 2] twice, cba, hdc in next stitch, turn.

Rows 6–8 Repeat Rows 2–4 of armhole shaping.

Shape Front Left Neck

Row 1 (RS) Ch 2, cba, [bpdc 2, cba] twice, hdc in next st, leave remaining stitches unworked, turn—12 stitches.

Row 2 Repeat Row 4 of Body.

Row 3 Ch 2, cba, [bpdc 2, cba] twice, hdc in next stitch, turn.

Row 4 Repeat Row 4 of Body.

Fasten off.

With RS facing, return to Row 8 of armhole shaping and sk 13 stitches, join yarn with a sl st to next stitch, repeat neck shaping for right shoulder. Fasten off.

Back

With RS facing, return to Row 8 of Body and sk 11 stitches, join yarn with a sl st in next stitch, repeat armhole and right and left neck shaping as for front. Fasten off.

Sleeve (make 2)

Ch 46.

Row 1 Dc in fourth chain from hook and in each chain across, turn—44 dc.

Row 2 Ch 2 (counts as hdc now and throughout), *bpdc, fpdc; repeat from * across ending with hdc in last stitch, turn.

Row 3 Ch 2, bpdc, [cba, bpdc 2] three times, fpdc, [bpdc 2, cba] three times, bpdc 2, fpdc, [bpdc 2, cba] three times, bpdc, hdc in last stitch, turn.

Row 4 Ch 2, fpdc around the post of every front raised stitch, bpdc around the post of every back raised stitch, hdc in last stitch, turn.

Row 5 Ch 2, bpdc, [cba, bpdc 2] three times, [cbc, cbb] four times, [bpdc 2, cba] three times, bpdc, hdc in last stitch, turn.

Row 6 Repeat Row 4 for sleeve.

Row 7 Ch 2, bpdc, [cba, bpdc 2] three times, bpdc, [cba, bpdc 2] four times, bpdc, [cba, bpdc 2] twice, cba, bpdc, hdc in last stitch, turn.

Row 8 Repeat Row 4 for sleeve.

Row 9 Ch 2, bpdc, [cba, bpdc 2] three times, [cbb, cbc] four times, [bpdc 2, cba] three times, bpdc, hdc in last stitch, turn.

Row 10 Repeat Row 4 for sleeve.

Fasten off.

Assembly

With right sides facing, seam left shoulder completely across, seam right shoulder stitching together only the first four stitches, starting at the armhole. Seam the sides. Set in sleeves. Join yarn to the neck at right front shoulder near the slit, sc evenly around neckline to the right back shoulder. Fasten off. Join the yarn to cuff of the sleeve, sc evenly around. Fasten off. Repeat for second sleeve. Turn sweater right side out. Attach button on right shoulder near slit at neck. Ch 7 to create loop, fasten off and attach securely opposite button.

abbreviations

Abbreviations in bold are explained in the Special Techniques section (page 11).

( )	work the instructions within parentheses as directed
*	work the instructions marked by asterisk(s) as directed
[ ]	work the instructions between the brackets as directed
"	inch(es)
approx	approximate
beg	beginning
bet	between
bl	**back loop(s)**
blo	**back loop only**
bpdc	**back post double crochet**
CA (B, C, D)	Color A (B, C, D)
ch	chain
ch-sp	chain-space
cm	centimeter(s)
cont	continue
dc	double crochet
dc2tog	double crochet two stitches together (a decrease)
dec	decrease
esc	**extended single crochet**
fl	**front loop(s)**
flo	**front loop only**
foll	following

fpdc	**front post double crochet**
fsc	**foundation single crochet**
g	gram
hdc	half double crochet
inc	increase
ldc	**linked double crochet**
lp(s)	loop(s)
m	meter(s)
oz	ounce(s)
pm	place marker
prev	previous
rem	remaining
rep	repeat(s)
rnd(s)	round(s)

RS	Right Side
sc	single crochet
sc2tog	single crochet 2 stitches together (a decrease)
sk	skip
sl st(s)	slip stitch(es)
sp(s)	space(s)
st(s)	stitches
tch	turning chain
tog	together
tr	treble crochet
WS	wrong side
yd(s)	yard(s)
yo	yarn over

abbreviation conversion chart

All abbreviations in this book are in U.S. format. Please refer to this chart if you need to convert the terms into UK/Australian format.

U. S. abbreviations		U. K. / Australian abbreviations	
dc	double crochet	tr	treble crochet
hdc	half double crochet	htr	half treble crochet
sc	single crochet	dc	double crochet
sl st	slip stitch	sc	single crochet
tr	treble crochet	dtr	double treble crochet

resources

Many of the yarns in this book were generously donated by the manufacturers. Others came from my local yarn shop here in Cordova, Alaska. In all cases I chose yarns based on their color, texture, and fiber content. You can read more about yarn choice and substitutions below. To learn about the yarns used in the book visit the manufacturers' websites:

Blue Sky Alpacas
www.blueskyalpacas.com

Brown Sheep
www.brownsheep.com

Cascade Yarns
www.cascadeyarns.com

Classic Elite
www.classiceliteyarns.com

DMC
www.dmc.com

Elmore Pisgah
www.elmore-pisgah.com

Knit One Crochet Too
www.knitonecrochettoo.com

Louet
www.louet.com

Malabrigo
www.malabrigoyarn.com

Mission Falls
www.missionfalls.com

O-Wool by Vermont Organic Fiber Company
www.owool.com

Patons
www.patonsyarns.com

Southwest Trading Company
www.soysilk.com
www.tofubear.com

hook sizes

U.S. Size	Metric Size
B-1	2.25mm
C-2	2.75mm
D-3	3.25mm
E-4	3.5mm
F-5	3.75mm
G-6	4mm
7	4.5mm
H-8	5mm
I-9	5.5mm
J-10	6mm
K-10½	6.5mm
L-11	8mm
M/N-13	9mm
N/P-15	10mm
P/Q	15mm
Q	16mm
S	19mm

Note that the small steel crochet hooks designed for thread crochet use the opposite sizing convention from the hooks listed above—the higher the number, the smaller the hook. Steel hooks range from size 14 (.9mm) to 00 (2.7mm). To avoid confusion, it's best to use the metric measurement when choosing hooks.

standard yarn weight system

Yarn weight symbol and category names	Superfine 1	Fine 2	Light 3	Medium 4	Bulky 5	Super Bulky 6
Type of Yarns in Category	Sock, Fingering, Baby	Sport, Baby	DK, Light Worsted	Worsted, Afghan, Aran	Chunky, Craft, Rug	Bulky, Roving
Crochet Gauge* Ranges in Single Crochet to 4 inch	21–32 sts	16–20 sts	12–17 sts	11–14 sts	8–11 sts	5–9 sts
Recommended Hook in Metric Size Range	2.25—3.5 mm	3.5—4.5 mm	4.5—5.5 mm	5.5—6.5 mm	6.5—9 mm	9 mm and larger
Recommended Hook U.S. Size Range	B-1 to E-4	E-4 to 7	7 to I-9	I-9 to K-10½	K-10½ to M-13	M-13 and larger

* GUIDELINES ONLY: The above reflect the most commonly used gauges and needle or hook sizes for specific yarn categories.

acknowledgments

Writing this book would not have been possible without the help and support of a number of wonderful people. I began work on this project just after arriving in Cordova, Alaska, a small, remote town that was a big change from beltway life in Maryland. Thank you so much to Dotty Widmann, owner of The Net Loft, our local yarn store, for welcoming me to town and setting me up with an instant community of fiber-lovers. Feeling at home here right away made working on the book much easier.

Thank you to Julie Armstrong Holetz who is the other half of my brain on so many of my projects and who provided sanity and technical editing for *Crochet for Bears to Wear*. Thank you to Amie Hirtes who interpreted my hand drawings to create the beautiful schematics and charts in the book. Thank you to my agent, Judy Heiblum, for her ongoing support and for her level head and clear thinking that bring me back to earth at the right times. Thank you to my editor, Rebecca Behan, for her insight and encouragement.

Thank you to all of the yarn companies that donated materials for the projects in this book: Elmore Pisgah, Brown Sheep, Cascade Yarns, Classic Elite, Knit One Crochet Too, O-Wool, and Blue Sky Alpacas. Thank you to Southwest Trading Company for donating yarn and the Tofu Bears, Eddie and Pearl.

Thank you to my family: Jay, Selma, and James, for their patience and support while I planned, crocheted, and wrote, and calculated, and wrote some more.

index

a

Abbreviations **92**
Adjustments to patterns **9**
Advanced patterns **9**
Amigurumi **17, 30**
  defined **31**
Arm length, measuring **8**

b

Back-loop crochet **12–13**
Back post double crochet (bpdc) **13**
Bat and Ball pattern **17**
Bear-y Pickin' Dress and Bonnet **17,
  32–35**
  bonnet details **34–35**
  custom-sized dress **35**
  dress details **33–34**
  salmonberry flowers **35**
Blocking your swatch **9**

c

Cable A stitch (cba) **89**
Cable B stitch (cbb) **89**
Cable C stitch (cbc) **89**
Calculator **15**
California Dreamin' Bikini **37, 42–45**
  custom-sized bikini bottom **45**
  custom-sized bikini top **44**
Carter, Belinda "Bendy" **63**
Chachula, Robyn **65**
Charts **10–11**
Circumference, measuring **8**
Clothes for bears projects **4**
Colors: changing in crochet project
  12
Copeland, Judith **25**
Cozy Turtleneck **73, 74–77**
Crochet on the Edge (Annie's Attic) **63**
Crochet pattern **8**
Customizing sidebars **4, 7–10**

d

Dolls, making clothes for **8**

e

Easy patterns **8**
Emborsky, Drew **13, 89**
Endless Summer Board Shorts **37,
  38–41**
  custom-sized **41**
  details **40**
Extended single crochet (esc) **13**

f

Fair Isle Sweater **12, 73, 78–81**
  custom-sized **81**
Finished measurements, comparing
  with toy's measurements **9**
Fisherman's Sweater **13, 73, 88–91**
Fly lure **49**
Foundation single crochet (fsc) **13**
Front-loop crochet **12–13**
Front post double crochet (fpdc) **13**

g

Gauge **9–10**
Gone Fishing Vest **37, 46–49**
  custom-sized **49**
Granite stitch **47–48**

h

Hat technique (basic), working
  in the round using **11**
Hook size **93**
  choosing **9**
Hooks **9**

i

Intermediate patterns **8–9**

k

Keim, Cecily **11**
Knits for Bears to Wear **5**

l

Let's Dance Ensemble **51, 64–71**
  custom-sized **69**
  Granny Motif **67**
Linked double crochet (ldc) **13, 61**
Long Winter's Nap Nightgown and
  Cap **73, 83–87**
  custom-sized night cap **86**
  custom-sized nightgown **85**

m

Measurements **7–8**
Measuring tape **15**
Modular crochet **25**

p

Patterns **4, 8–11**
  adjustments to **9–10**
Pins **15**
Post stitches **12–13**

r

Removable stitch markers **15**
Resources **93**

s

Schematics **10–11**
Schoolgirl Pleated Skirt and Beret
  51, 60–63

box pleats **63**
Scissors **15**
7th Inning Stretch Baseball Jersey
  and Cap **17, 24–31**
  custom-sized baseball cap **28**
  custom-sized baseball jersey **27**
  home run bat and ball **30–31**
Show Your Colors Varsity Jacket **51,
  52–57**
  book bag **57–59**
  custom-sized **56**
Sizing differences **9–10**
Southwest Trading Company **5, 94**
Special techniques **11**
Spiraled rounds **12**
Spring Cleaning Jeans and T-Shirt
  17, 18–23
  custom-sized jeans **22–23**
  custom-sized T-shirt **20–21**
Standard yarn weight system **93**
Stitch gauge, taking measurements
  of **9, 10**
Swatch **9**

t

Teach Yourself Visually: Crochet
  (Werker/Keim) **11**
Tools **14–15**

w

Werker, Kim **11**
Working in the round **11–12**

y

Yarn **14–15**
  choosing **9**
Yarn needle **15**

Published in the United States by Potter Craft,
an imprint of the Crown Publishing Group,
a division of Random House, Inc., New York.

www.crownpublishing.com
www.pottercraft.com

POTTER CRAFT and colophon is a registered
trademark of Random House, Inc.

Library of Congress Cataloging-in-Publication Data
Houck, Amy O'Neill.

  Crochet for bears to wear : more than 20 perfect projects
for your favorite teddies and friends / by Amy O'Neill Houck.
     p. cm.
  Includes index.
  ISBN 978-0-307-46212-1
  1. Crochet--Patterns. 2. Doll clothes--Patterns. 3. Teddy
bears. I. Title.
  TT825.H676 2010
  746.43'4041--dc22
                            2009034317

Printed in China

Design by Chi Ling Moy
Photography by Jennifer Lévy

10 9 8 7 6 5 4 3 2 1

First Edition

𝓣𝓱𝓪𝓷𝓴𝓼 to the Craft Yarn Council of America
(www.yarnstandards.com) for their Standard
Yarn Weight System Chart and hook size information,
page 93.